CHINA:
REVOLUTION AND
COUNTERREVOLUTION

PSL PUBLICATIONS

SAN FRANCISCO

China: Revolution and Counterrevolution

The contents were originally released in January 2008
as part of the *Socialism and Liberation* journal series.

Library of Congress Control Number: 2012930231
ISBN: 978-0-9841220-9-7
Printed in the United States

Contributors
Brian Becker, Heather Benno, Nathalie Hrizi,
Gloria La Riva, Eugene Puryear, Sarah Sloan and others

Technical Editor
Keith Pavlik

PSL Publications
2969 Mission Street, Suite 200
San Francisco, CA 94110
(415) 821-6171
books@PSLweb.org
www.PSLweb.org

China: Revolution and Counterrevolution

Contents continued on next page

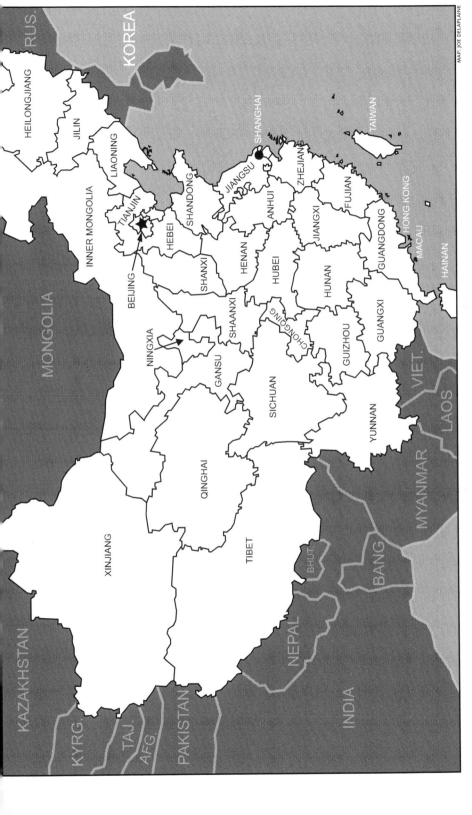

A chronology of class struggle in China

1839-42: First Opium War. British imported tea from China, and in return exported opium from India into China. In 1839, the Chinese government destroys 20,000 chests of British opium and prohibits its use. Britain retaliates militarily.

1842: Treaty of Nanjing. The Chinese, defeated by the British military in the Opium War, are forced to sign the Treaty of Nanjing. China is forced to give Hong Kong to the British and open five ports for the British to inhabit and in which to conduct trade, including opium. The British are also exempted from Chinese law.

1851-64: Taiping Rebellion is led by Hong Xiuquan, a village teacher. Millions of peasants join the fight against the Qing government. British and French forces, preferring to deal with the weakened Qing administration, support it against the rebels. An estimated 30 million people are killed in the rebellion.

1883-85: France defeats China in the Franco-Chinese war, gaining control of nearby Indochina. Britain extends its empire from India to Burma.

1893: Mao Zedong is born.

1894-95: The Sino-Japanese war ends in a Chinese defeat. China is forced to give Formosa (Taiwan) to Japan and to relinquish claims on Korea. This begins a half-century of Japanese colonial domination of Korea.

1898: Spanish-American War. United States takes over Spanish colonies of Puerto Rico, Cuba, Guam and the Philippines. The Philippines is used as a base for U.S. penetration of China.

1899: The U.S. government announces the "Open Door Policy," calling for an equal opportunity for foreign powers to "develop" China for their own commercial interests. The policy is implemented because nearly all of China's coastal region has been taken over by six other imperialist powers.

1900: The Boxer Rebellion. Starting in northern China, people attack missionary facilities and Chinese Christians. By June 1900, militants besiege the foreign invaders in Beijing and Tianjin. The Qing government supports the militants against the foreigners, but the Chinese are crushed by British firepower. Reprisals include mass executions, forced payment of money to the foreigners and the stationing of foreign troops on Chinese soil.

1911: The Republican Revolution, also known as the First Revolution, signals the end of the Manchu Dynasty in Central and South China. Dr. Sun Yat-sen is declared president of a provisional government in Nanking.

1912: Sun Yat-sen resigns and Yuan Shih-k'ai becomes president of the Republic of China. Over the next few years, he suspends the provisional constitution and parliament, declares himself emperor, and is overthrown in 1916.

1914-18: World War I. Japan, allied with Britain and France, seizes German holdings in Shandong province in 1914. In 1917, Britain, France and Italy secretly support Japanese control over southeastern Manchuria and eastern Inner Mongolia.

1917: The October Revolution is victorious in Russia. The new revolutionary Russian government supports the Kuomintang—the National People's Party—founded by Dr. Sun Yat-sen.

1921: The Communist Party of China is formed. Mao Zedong is named secretary of the Communist Party of Hunan province.

1923: Members of the CPC join the Kuomintang as individuals, forming the first "united front."

1925-27: Revolutionary upsurge in China.

1925: Advisers from the Communist International (Comintern) support Chiang Kai-shek as military leader of the Nationalist Revolutionary Expedition, launched from Canton in 1926. The Comintern helps establish Whampoa Military Academy to train Chinese officers.

1927: Forces loyal to Chiang Kai-shek attack the urban-based CPC in an anti-communist coup. The CPC loses 80 percent of its members in the attacks, its numbers dwindling to about 10,000. Surviving CPC members retreat to the countryside.

Mao Zedong leads peasants in the unsuccessful Autumn Harvest Uprising in Hunan province. The Red Army is founded.

1929-30: Chiang Kai-shek launches first of five "final extermination" campaigns against CPC base areas. The first four campaigns would be defeated.

1931: Japan invades Manchuria, China's main industrial region, and sets up the puppet state of "Manchukuo."

1932: Japan attacks Shanghai.

1934-35: The Long March. Chiang Kai-shek's massive "Fifth Final Extermination" campaign forces the CPC and Red Army to embark on the Long March, which lasts for more than a year. Traveling thousands of miles on foot and fighting numerous battles, the communist-led forces suffer heavy losses but survive and establish a new base area in Yenan.

1937: Japan launches a massive invasion of China. The CPC proposes a united front strategy to fight Japanese invaders. Chiang Kai-shek only agrees after being kidnapped and held hostage by his own generals. The war continues against Japanese invaders until 1945.

1940-41: Cooperation between CPC and Kuomintang forces breaks down. The Kuomintang relies on U.S. aid, and the communists expand their guerrilla movement.

1941-45: 27 million Soviet workers and peasants are killed in Word War II. Two-thirds of the Soviet Union's industry is destroyed.

1945: The CPC has 1.2 million members, up from 100,000 in 1937.

1946: The CPC renames the Red Army the People's Liberation Army.

1948: The communists overwhelmingly defeat Chiang Kai-shek's Nationalist forces in Manchuria despite massive U.S. aid.

1949: The People's Liberation Army defeats the Kuomintang in the Hwai-hai campaign in January.

On Oct. 1, the People's Republic of China is formally declared. Chiang Kai-shek flees to Taiwan. A People's Political Consultative Conference is held, based on Mao's text, "The People's Democratic Dictatorship." Workers, peasants, intellectuals and the national bourgeoisie are represented. Mao is elected chairman. He announces a foreign policy of "leaning to one side"—toward the Soviet Union. The People's Republic of China is recognized by several countries: the Soviet Union, Norway, Finland, Sweden, Switzerland, the Netherlands and Great Britain. The United States withdraws its diplomats from China. CPC membership reaches 4.5 million.

1950: China and the Soviet Union sign a treaty of alliance. An agrarian reform law redistributes land from the landlords to the peasants. The new marriage law gives greater rights to women. The People's Liberation Army enters the Tibetan area of Chamdo.

War breaks out in Korea after United Nations forces, led by the United States, are sent to the peninsula.

Chinese troops fight on the side of the Democratic People's Republic of Korea (North Korea). The U.S. government sends the Navy to "protect" Taiwan.

1951: Chinese representatives in Beijing present Tibetan representatives with a Seventeen Point Agreement affirming China's sovereignty over Tibet. The agreement is ratified in Lhasa a few months later.

1953: China's first Five-Year Plan is announced. Using the Soviet Union's economic plans as a model, China's plan calls for heavy industrial development. Soviet aid and advisers assist in implementation. An armistice is signed in the Korean War, but no formal peace treaty is ever signed.

1955: Major industries are socialized. China and the Soviet Union reach an agreement on nuclear cooperation.

1956: China backs the Soviet intervention to put down a counter-revolutionary rebellion in Hungary.

1958: The second Five-Year Plan—known as the "Great Leap Forward"—begins. This includes the introduction of the people's commune as the basic unit of economic life in the Chinese countryside, part of a widespread collectivization effort. The goal is to rapidly industrialize China by mobilizing the country's vast peasant population behind the effort.

1959: The Soviet Union repudiates a secret agreement to assist China in developing nuclear weapons. Soviet leader Nikita Khrushchev visits the United States for three days of private talks with President Dwight D. Eisenhower. Following the failure of a reactionary armed uprising in Tibet, the Dalai Lama flees to India to establish a new "government in exile."

1960: Ideological differences between China and the Soviet Union lead to a split. Khrushchev had denounced Joseph Stalin after Stalin's death and called for co-existence between communist and capitalist countries. The Soviet Union recalls all technical advisers from China and cancels more than 600 contracts between the two countries.

1962: Border disputes and incidents between India and China escalate, centered on a disputed area in which China had constructed a military road to Tibet. China attacks, taking 35,000 square miles of territory, but then unilaterally retreats, creating a demilitarized zone and calling for peaceful negotiations to resolve the dispute.

1962-65: The Socialist Education Movement is launched to combat bourgeois tendencies within the CPC. Classes are scheduled to fit the work schedules of factories and communes. Intellectuals are drafted to do manual labor.

1963: The Soviet Union signs a partial nuclear test ban treaty with the United States and Britain.

1964: China condemns U.S. aggression against Vietnam, saying that an attack on Vietnam is like an attack on China itself. China successfully tests its first atomic bomb.

1965: Counterrevolution in Indonesia overthrows the bourgeois-nationalist government of Sukarno, a key ally of China. Over 1 million Indonesian communists and their supporters are massacred.

1966: The Great Proletarian Cultural Revolution is launched by Mao and other leaders within the CPC. In many ways, it is a struggle between left and more right-wing leaders over the course China will take, and a struggle against entrenched party bureaucrats and bourgeois tendencies. The Sino-Soviet split escalates from a mainly ideological struggle to a state-to-state conflict.

1967: In January and February, workers in Shanghai establish the "Shanghai Commune."

1968: Mao announces a directive, by which educated urban youth will work in the countryside for re-education with poor peasants. There are numerous clashes, some involving casualties, between China and the Soviet Union along their border; these clashes continue the next year.

1968: China denounces the Soviet intervention to block counterrevolution in Czechoslovakia as a manifestation of "Soviet social imperialism."

1969: Cultural Revolution left-wing leader and People's Liberation Army commander Lin Biao is designated as constitutional successor to Mao Zedong. Lin had authored (in 1965) an article, "Long Live the Victory of the People's War!" outlining a worldwide strategy of anti-imperialist struggle and had compiled the "Quotations from Chairman Mao Zedong," which became known as "the Little Red Book."

1970: China launches its first satellite into orbit.

1971: President Richard Nixon's national security advisor, Henry Kissinger, secretly visits Beijing during a trip to Pakistan in July.

1971: Lin Biao dies in a mysterious plane crash in September. Chen Boda, another prominent leftist leader, drops from public view.

The People's Republic of China takes its rightful seat at the United Nations after a majority of member nations demand it.

1972: President Nixon visits China in February as a further step toward a U.S.-China rapprochement. During Nixon's stay, the United States and China issue the Shanghai Communiqué. The document pledges that the countries will work to normalize their relations. The U.S. government formally recognizes the principle that Taiwan is a part of China.

1976: In January, Chinese premier Zhou Enlai dies. Deng Xiaoping is purged from CPC leadership positions in April.

In September, Mao Zedong dies. Key leftist allies of Mao, the "Gang of Four," are arrested in October.

1977: Deng Xiaoping is restored to his CPC positions.

1978: Deng Xiaoping signals a reorganization of the Chinese economy, which he describes as "socialism with Chinese characteristics." The Third Plenum of the 11th CPC Congress emphasizes the need for economic modernization with a focus on industry, agriculture, defense and science/technology.

Following multiple incursions by Pol Pot forces into Vietnam, Vietnamese troops intervene in Cambodia in December, overthrowing the China-allied Khmer Rouge regime.

1979: The United States and China resume full diplomatic relations on January 1. Four months later, the U.S. government passes the Taiwan Relations Act, formalizing quasi-diplomatic relations between the United States and Taiwan. China solidifies a strategic alliance with the United States against the Soviet Union and its allies.

China invades Vietnam on Feb. 17, partly in response to Vietnam's occupation of Cambodia. Chinese troops withdraw three weeks later.

1980: China designates four economic zones open to foreign investors and relaxes restrictions on foreign investors.

1982: The new Chinese Constitution enshrines the market.

1985: Time magazine names Deng Xiaoping "Man of the Year" for his embrace of "free-market reforms."

1989: From April to June, demonstrators occupy Tiananmen Square in Beijing, opposing the government. Demands escalate from calling for "democracy" to calling for the CPC-led government to resign. Protests continue for six weeks before the government moves to end them. Several hundred people die in fights near the square on June 3-4, many of whom were soldiers of the

People's Liberation Army. Anti-China hysteria sweeps the United States. The U.S.-China alliance ends.

Eastern European socialist governments in Poland, East Germany, Hungary, Czechoslovakia, Bulgaria and Romania are overthrown.

1990-91: The United States invades Iraq in January 1991. China votes in the United Nations to abstain, in effect giving the United States a green light for the invasion.

1991: The Soviet Union is overthrown and dismantled.

1992: The 14th CPC Congress declares its intent to build a "socialist market economy." Major Chinese cities are opened to foreign investment.

1996: China holds missile tests off Taiwan.

1997: In February, Deng Xiaoping dies.

Hong Kong is returned to China, ending 155 years of British colonial rule.

1999: NATO warplanes bomb the Chinese Embassy in Yugoslavia during the war.

2000: The U.S. Senate passes the Permanent Normal Trade Relations bill, which guarantees Chinese goods the same access to the U.S. market as products from other countries.

2001: In April, a U.S. spy plane collides with a Chinese fighter jet, killing the Chinese pilot and forcing the spy plane to land on the southern Chinese island of Hainan. China accuses the U.S. plane of ramming its aircraft.

China joins the World Trade Organization in November.

2002: The 16th National Congress of the CPC opens party membership to China's capitalists—owners of private capital.

2003: The United States invades and occupies Iraq.

2004: China's global trade exceeds $1 trillion, becoming the third largest trading country behind the United States and Germany.

2005: The United States and Japan issue a joint agreement in February, declaring for the first time that security in the Taiwan Strait is a "common strategic objective." The declaration is a thinly veiled threat against China.

China Reform Forum chair Zheng Bijian states that the number one goal of the country's leadership is for China to go from being an "underdeveloped" country to a "medium-level developed country" by the mid-21st century.

2006: China joins the unanimous U.N. Security Council vote sanctioning Iran for its uranium enrichment program.

2007: In May, Nigeria launches its first telecommunications satellite from China. It was designed and built by Chinese engineers.

In June, China's National People's Congress adopts a labor reform bill over the objection of the international capitalists requiring employers to provide workers with written contracts including long-term job security provisions.

Seventeen members of the CPC issue a public letter in July to the CPC's leadership, urging a reconsideration of the general line of economic reforms.

The United States, in October, awards the Dalai Lama the congressional gold medal—the government's highest civilian honor.

In November, China blocks U.S. naval vessels from entering Hong Kong, saying that relations with the United States have been "disturbed and harmed" because of actions with regard to Tibet and recent massive weapons sales to Taiwan.

CHINA:
REVOLUTION AND
COUNTERREVOLUTION

What do socialists defend in China today?

BY BRIAN BECKER

For almost two years, members of the Party for Socialism and Liberation undertook an internal educational campaign, discussion and review of the current government of the People's Republic of China from the perspective of the struggle for socialism and the interests of the world working class. This discussion was in preparation for the possibility of a major struggle—waged from within and without—against the Chinese government, which is led by the Communist Party of China.

The following article is a summary of that discussion. The formal PSL resolution adopted by the party's National Committee, including a thorough review of the history of the Chinese Revolution and Mao Zedong's struggle against the elements known as "capitalist roaders," is included as an appendix (see page 175).

THE 17th National Congress of the Communist Party of China closed in October 2007. Its final summary resolution restated the ruling party's goal of building "socialism with Chinese characteristics," although it claims that China "is still in the primary stage of socialism."[1]

When Frederick Engels outlined the goal of the fledgling communist movement in 1847, he noted that communism will be achieved "by the elimination of private property and its replacement by community of property."[2] Engels, like Marx, identified the abolition of private property as a foundational feature for the transition from class society to communism.

He further explained: "The abolition of private ownership is indeed the most succinct and characteristic summary of the transformation of the entire social system necessarily following from the development of industry, and it is therefore rightly put forward by the Communists as their main demand."[3]

By that definition, it is clear that the road taken by the Communist Party of China since 1978, following the death of Mao Zedong and the defeat of his supporters within the CPC, has been in the opposite direction from communism—notwithstanding all the party's public declarations.

The 1949 Chinese Revolution placed China squarely on the path toward socialist development. While elements of that revolution remain, the country and the ruling social order have dynamically moved toward the restoration of capitalist property relations.

Capitalist private property has been legalized and encouraged. Tens of thousands of privately owned enterprises co-exist along with state-owned enterprises. The official monopoly of foreign trade has been gradually reduced, with many of the largest western transnational capitalist corporations and banks setting up operations in cities throughout China. Large numbers of Chinese workers are employed by these foreign firms, producing vast surplus value for western investors. The Chinese government considers this to be a necessary development strategy.[4]

That is not to say that private capital—or foreign capital in particular—has the decisive upper hand in the Chinese economy. The gradual dissolution of the monopoly of foreign trade obscures the still-powerful mediating role of the Communist Party-led state that acts to safeguard China's evolving industrial and scientific apparatus from the encroachments of western imperialist corporations.

There are some recent signs that the Chinese state is increasing restrictions on foreign capital so as to safeguard the position of Chinese enterprises. Each move in this direction sets off alarms among western capitalists.

The New York Times reported in November 2007: "'There is clearly a growing economic nationalism in China that is leading to discrimination against foreign investors in pillar sectors of the economy,' said Myron Brilliant, vice president for Asia at the United States Chamber of Commerce. 'It's not only a threat to foreign investors but it also undermines China's transition to a market-based economy.'"[5]

Given that it is the Communist Party itself that inaugurated the restoration of capitalist property relations and opened the country to foreign transnational corporations, does the party's hold on state power in China really matter? Or is the Communist Party of China's continued political control over the government essentially the same as the political control of any ruling political party in a capitalist country?

Has the adoption of a market-driven economy eviscerated all that was achieved by China's socialist revolution? And conversely, if the CPC loses political power, are there foreseeable negative consequences for the Chinese working class and peasantry in a country that is still emerging from the cruel legacy of underdevelopment?

It is our assertion that if the overthrow of the Communist Party of China were carried out by forces of domestic counterrevolution—forces that would be vigorously supported by U.S. imperialism—it would represent a historic setback for China.

It is our assertion that if the overthrow of the Communist Party of China were carried out by forces of domestic counterrevolution, it would represent a historic setback for China.

The negative consequences of such an overthrow by any force other than a revolutionary communist party would fall into two broad categories. First, China's dynamic forward economic development would come to a screeching halt. The country would be re-enslaved by the forces of western neo-colonialism—and very possibly dismembered as a national entity, as happened in the course of counterrevolution in the Soviet Union, Czechoslovakia and Yugoslavia.

Secondly, the overthrow of the CPC would culminate the process of capitalist restoration in China. Although the restoration of capitalism is currently a process that is far advanced, it is still unfinished. The CPC's continued hold on political power leaves open the possibility, however remote, that the present pro-capitalist course can be slowed, halted and even reversed.

If the Communist Party of China were to be replaced by another party or group dedicated to the transition to socialism and communism, repudiating the "capitalist road" reforms of the past 29 years, that would be a welcome development. No such development is apparent in the near future.

The starting point for any socialist or progressive person who honestly hopes for China's return to a revolutionary socialist orientation must be where the pro-communist forces in China can be found. Any left wing and truly pro-communist forces that exist in China are almost certainly located within the 73 million members of the CPC, not in some other political formation.

OVERVIEW OF CHINA'S REVOLUTION

The 1949 Chinese Revolution took place in an economic landscape far different than that envisaged by the founders of scientific socialism, Karl Marx and Frederick Engels, in the late 1840s. Marx and Engels foresaw the proletarian or socialist revolution taking place first in industrially advanced capitalist countries. They believed that the success of building socialism would be possible based on the revolutionary movement initially succeeding in at least two or more industrially advanced countries, which would then allow for economic cooperation.[6]

China's socialist revolution took place in an impoverished country with a predominantly peasant population. China was rife with mass starvation and famine. The Chinese people lived under the humiliating boot of western imperialism, facing mass opium addiction promoted by British colonialism. The people had withstood 22 years of fierce countrywide civil war and 15 years of Japanese military occupation.

Given this backdrop, the sheer heroism of the Chinese Revolution was breathtaking in scope. The leadership, especially Mao Zedong, had to navigate a path to revolution through the most complex and difficult problems. It is a truly amazing, larger-than-life story of human beings forging together a communist party and uniting hundreds of millions of destitute workers, peasants and peoples from many nationalities who together overcame the brutality of war and repression.

China's revolution was socialist in the sense that its leaders in the CPC had a socialist orientation toward fulfilling the historic interests of the working class—even though the working class itself was still relatively small and immature. The old capitalist state was smashed, and the ruling Nationalist Party (Kuomintang) army led by Chiang Kai-shek fled the mainland for Taiwan.

The revolution created a new state—a new instrument of coercion against the former ruling class based on a new class power.

The communist-led Red Army, made up of millions of peasants and workers, became the anchor of the new state power. The workers and poor peasants were elevated, at least in a sociological sense, to be the new ruling power.

Between 1949 and 1955, the Chinese people—with the leadership of what appeared on the surface to be a unified Communist Party—eradicated mass starvation, opium addiction and prostitution. They made huge advances toward wiping out illiteracy, providing health care for the hundreds of millions of people and stable employment for the urban working class. Landlordism was eradicated in the countryside. Social change of this character was virtually unprecedented in history. By 1955, core industries had been nationalized and the beginnings of a planned economy began to take shape.

TWIN TASKS OF THE CHINESE REVOLUTION

Despite the Chinese Revolution's socialist character, many of the tasks that had been accomplished in the process of the bourgeois democratic revolutions in Europe were unaddressed in China as of 1949. The flourishing of modern industry, urbanization and the dissolution of the patriarchal village, the break-up of feudal estates, separation of church and state, the ascendancy of science, formal and legally recognized individual rights—these characteristic features of the bourgeois democratic revolution were undone tasks as of 1949.

These basic historical tasks had been thwarted in China by the combined forces of western imperialism, operating in and through their Chinese proxies, the semi-feudal dynastic establishment, and the comprador capitalist ruling class. Despite Marx and Engels' original prognostications, the Chinese communists led a social revolution under circumstances far different from those that existed in the west.

The inter-tangled bourgeois and socialist revolutions, with historically contradictory tasks, appeared at the same juncture in China's transformation. The CPC, in turn, although its true base was the revolutionary peasantry and urban working class, would ultimately become the political chamber where various and conflicting class currents competed for influence.

China's development since the revolution is filled with a historical irony: The period of socialist tasks, roughly corresponding to the years

1950-78, has since 1978 been replaced by a period where the bourgeois task of national capitalist development has been primary. This is the reverse of what the earliest communist theorists had anticipated.

The same economic backwardness that retarded the growth of the working class also stunted the growth of the bourgeoisie in China. In Europe, the vanguard sectors of the bourgeoisie became a revolutionary force against feudalism and the nobility of medieval Europe. Ironically, it fell to the Chinese workers' and peasants' revolution to sever the debilitating connection to western imperialism. This, in turn, was the prerequisite for the elimination of semi-feudalism and comprador capitalism. By reclaiming the sovereignty of the country China was able to rapidly address the tasks of the bourgeois democratic revolution.

The process by which the leadership of China's bourgeois democratic revolution fell to the working class and the communist party is succinctly described by William Hinton, the author of "Fanshen," the classic study of village life in post-revolutionary China.

> China's independent national bourgeoisie, the revolutionary sector of the bourgeois class, was weak and vacillating. It could not possibly take on both the Chinese landlords and the imperialists plus their Chinese comprador partners without fully mobilizing both the working class and the peasantry. But mobilizing the working class meant putting certain limits on managerial powers and meeting certain working-class demands—job security, retirement pay, and health care—while mobilizing the peasantry meant carrying out land reform. This could not be done without confiscating the wealth of the landlord class, from which the bourgeoisie had, in the main, arisen and to which it still maintained myriad ties. Furthermore, the confiscation of property and land threatened the foundations of all private property and caused capitalists—much as they desired liberation from feudalism and imperialism—to vacillate. Over and over again, the national bourgeoisie proved incapable of firm national leadership against the people's enemies, foreign and

domestic. Leading the Chinese democratic revolution thus shifted by default to the working class, more numerous by far and older and more experienced than the bourgeoisie, and to the Communist Party that had established itself as spokesman for all the oppressed.[7]

THE RUSSIAN EXPERIENCE

It was not the first time the historic tasks of the bourgeois democratic and socialist revolutions were combined. The process of combined and uneven development explains the reality not only for China's development but also for Russia's at the time of its socialist revolution in 1917. Lenin, writing in 1899 about the future path of the revolution in backward and semi-feudal Russia, came to the conclusion that the stifling of Russia's democratic revolution would lead to the working class—rather than the liberal bourgeoisie—becoming the vanguard of a revolution that he still believed would be essentially bourgeois democratic in character.[8]

After the 1917 Russian Revolution, the new revolutionary government inherited a capitalist economy that was brutally backward. It had less than one-twelfth the level of U.S. economic output. The Russian people were largely illiterate peasants using tools of production that were a century behind those in the advanced capitalist world.

Yet during the 1930s—when the industrially advanced capitalist economies of the United States and Western Europe were paralyzed by the Great Depression—the Soviet planned economy experienced tempestuous rates of industrial growth. Having removed private ownership and the anarchy of a system of production chasing profits in the "market," the Soviets experienced a labor shortage rather than mass unemployment.

In fact, with the exception of the years of the German invasion during World War II, the Soviet planned economy avoided any period of economic recession or depression. Its economy had full employment—unemployment was nonexistent. Even in the years between 1978 and 1990, when Soviet economic growth slowed dramatically, it did not fall into the negative growth that characterizes economic recession.

By comparison with the United States, England, France, Germany, Japan and the other imperialist and colonizing countries, the standard of living of the Soviet worker was relatively low. But compared with Russia's pre-1917 quality of life—not to mention the quality of life of workers in the oppressed countries of Latin America, Africa and Asia—Soviet workers experienced a much higher standard of living by any measure.

WHAT IS A WORKERS' STATE?

In fact, the experience of the first socialist revolution in Russia helped communists around the world learn, in practice, the necessary measures for building a society free from capitalist exploitation in a world dominated by imperialism.

Four basic features of the Soviet Union constituted the foundation for the Soviet workers' state, which, despite bureaucratic flaws and deformities, distinguished it as a viable and superior social system in comparison to the capitalist system that preceded it in Russia.

First, the state and government were created following the smashing of the old state power of the bourgeoisie by a revolution of the workers and peasants. Second, there was public ownership of the means of production. Third, there was centralized economic planning rather than the commodity market as the engine driving economic production—production for needs instead of private profit. Fourth, the government administered a monopoly of foreign trade, preventing world imperialism from linking up with local Russian capitalists to create a "fifth column" within Soviet society.

These objective criteria help to explain what makes the workers' state fundamentally different from a traditional bourgeois state, which is a state that exists to defend capitalist interests against other potentially threatening classes that are oppressed by the capitalists. Marx and Lenin understood, however, that the workers' state in the early stage of socialism was not a pure workers' organization. To the extent that the new state's laws and enforcement mechanisms defended a system that allowed for inequality in the distribution of the economic and social surplus, it retained vestiges of a "bourgeois state but without a bourgeoisie."[9]

During most of its 74 years, the Soviet Union maintained these four key features that shaped the economic system constructed following the 1917 workers' and peasants' revolution. They distinguished the Soviet economic system from the capitalist mode of production.

That is not to say that the Soviet Union's economy represented a fully developed socialist system. On the contrary, it could be argued that the Soviet Union never evolved past the very first stage of socialist "social relations." There was inequality and many holdovers from centuries of underdevelopment. But the Soviet Union was clearly functioning according to an economic mechanism that was far different from capitalism, where the market and production are based on private bourgeois profit.

Using these preliminary socialist economic methods, the Soviet Union developed into the second-largest economy in the world. It eliminated unemployment. The Soviet system had no need for an industrial reserve army of the unemployed because production was no longer based on squeezing surplus value out of the working class. The paramount requirement of satisfying the profit needs of the capitalist and investor class was gone because the capitalists were deposed as a ruling class.

The Soviet Union did not just grow into a major world power. Soviet workers and peasants achieved unheard of social and economic rights and benefits. These rights were legal rights guaranteed by the state—a sharp contrast to the capitalist state, which defends first and foremost the right of capital to exploit labor. For the first time in history, the so-called "rule of law" was applied to the needs of the oppressed class for employment, housing, health care, education, child care, recreation and relaxation.

PHASES OF THE CHINESE REVOLUTION

The contradictions caused by the impact of China's socialist revolution taking place in a social environment that pre-dated the bourgeois democratic revolution imprinted themselves on all the political and factional struggles within the CPC following 1949. As Karl Marx noted in "The Eighteenth Brumaire of Louis Bonaparte" in 1852: "[People] make their own history, but they do not make it just as they please … but under circumstances directly encountered, given and transmitted from the past."[10]

The 1949 seizure of state power by the communists in China did not eliminate class conflict. In assessing the problems faced by the new revolutionary regime, the starting point is the existence of classes and strata of workers, peasants, large landowners, and big and small capitalists.

The expropriation of the big capitalists between 1952 and 1955, the establishment of socialist planning for economic production and distribution, and the establishment of a state-based monopoly of foreign trade served a twofold function. First, China reclaimed its economic and political sovereignty and independence—expressed most succinctly in Mao's first speech in 1949 at Tiananmen Square, when he announced that "China has stood up." Second, society and its productive powers were placed at the disposal of the individual and social needs of the workers and peasants of China, who had emerged as the new ruling class.

All these factors corresponded to the sociological definition of a workers' state that had emerged following the experience of the Soviet Union.

The communists of China could take power, but they could not immediately make China ready to rapidly progress toward communism and a classless society. Communism presupposes vast material

Counterrevolution would mean a return to the days of mass starvation and poverty. Here, Chinese peasants demand food in 1938.

abundance and the elimination of scarcity. Society must not only be able to provide all the food, clothing and shelter necessary to distribute "to each according to their need."[11] The industrial, scientific, transport and communications apparatus must also be able to produce industrial and consumer goods in such abundance that not only are immediate human needs satisfied but society has the wherewithal to continue on a path of dynamic and ecologically sustainable economic development.

In the case of an underdeveloped country, whose assets and prospective wealth have been siphoned off for the enrichment of foreign investors, the issue of building socialism is additionally complicated. Income redistribution and nationalized property present themselves as coinciding tasks after the revolution in the relatively "affluent" imperialist countries. In a poor country like China, underdeveloped because of colonialism and semi-colonialism, the task is to find a path of economic development that begins the process of the primary accumulation of the means of production.

That problem was compounded by the absence of adequate public education and a weak scientific and industrial infrastructure, creating the phenomena of mass illiteracy and a work force untrained for the task of taking over the management of the factories, mines, and the transport and communications apparatus. Thus, the privileged classes who were favored with greater opportunity for training and education in the old society become sorely needed as the "experts" by the new socialist regime.

Immediately after its victory in 1949, the leadership of the Communist Party, by necessity, focused on the question of China's economic development. Affecting the day-to-day lives of more than 500 million people, no task was more urgent than economic and social development. On this all wings of the Communist Party agreed.

How this development would take place in the context of the continued class struggle, however, became the pivot for what became known in China as the "two-line struggle" between elements of the party centered around Mao Zedong and those led by Liu Shaoqi and Deng Xiaoping. The Mao grouping advocated socialist methods for development, including nationalized public property in the core industries and banking, centralized planning, collectivized agriculture, mobilization of the workers and peasants, and a monopoly of foreign trade. The wing led by Liu and Deng was essentially pragmatic rather than Marxist in their approach, utilizing material incentives, capitalist-style accounting methods and elements of the capitalist market— all while professing allegiance to the goal of building socialism.

In 1966, this struggle led to the Great Proletarian Cultural Revolution, a mass campaign initiated by Mao and his allies that aimed to rally the poor and the young to dislodge from positions of authority Liu, Deng and thousands of others castigated as favoring the "capitalist road" for China's economic development.

Contrary to the presentation by bourgeois historians, the two-line struggle was not primarily over the pace of economic development in China, with Mao favoring a slower approach and Liu and Deng favoring a faster tempo. Both sides in the two-line struggle put the rapid economic development of China as a top priority.

> In assessing the problems faced by the new revolutionary regime, the starting point is the existence of classes and strata of workers, peasants, large landowners, and big and small capitalists.

In fact, the Chinese economy increased at a breakneck pace during the Mao era. Industrial output increased at an annual rate of 11.2 percent between 1952 and Mao's death in 1976. Even during the most intensive upheavals and disruptions to production caused by the civil strife associated with the Cultural Revolution, industrial production grew at an annual average rate of 10 percent.[12] This was done with almost no foreign aid or assistance. Soviet economic aid, assistance and advisors had been withdrawn by 1961 in the wake of the Sino-Soviet split. China received few international bank loans.

While China's tenfold increase in industrial production during the Mao era was a stunning advance, the progress in the impoverished rural villages and countryside was significantly slower. Overall agricultural production increased twofold during the same period.

Although the annual living standards among the rural population only increased by about 1 percent during the 1952-76 period,[13] Chinese peasants enjoyed huge advances in public health, free public education, affordable housing and social security as a result of collectivization and the commune system. The extreme cleavage between rich and poor in the countryside was reduced. Although the growth in agriculture lacked the tempestuous growth of the industrial sector, it is noteworthy that "China grew 30-40 percent more food than India on 14 percent less arable land than India" during the same time period.[14]

Despite the historic achievements on the road to socialism during this period, a series of international events and their reflection within the Communist Party weakened the strength of the revolutionary wing of the party. The defeat of the Indonesian Revolution in 1965, the escalation of the Sino-Soviet split and the ultimate rapprochement between China and U.S. imperialism, the corresponding death of People's Liberation Army leader Lin Biao, and the purge of other leftists—all these events laid the basis for the reemergence of the "capitalist road" grouping following Mao's death in 1976.

At the time, some observers of the Chinese Revolution considered the accusation that certain party leaders were "capitalist roaders" to be one more rhetorical flourish or excess of the Cultural Revolution. But the accusation, as it turned out, was not overheated rhetoric at all. It was a precise and accurate description of Mao's political opponents inside the leadership of the Communist Party.

Following Mao's death in 1976, the left wing of the party was routed and its leaders were arrested. By 1978, the "capitalist roaders," galvanized under the leadership of Deng Xiaoping, introduced sweeping economic reforms under the newly concocted and theoretically unfounded label of "market socialism."

These reforms led over the course of several steps to the "opening up" of China to imperialist banks and corporations. The development strategy was premised on a strategic assumption: The lure of super profits from the employment of low-wage labor in China would lead to massive capital investment by the industries and banks that possessed the most advanced technology. China would benefit in its "development" by accessing and acquiring the latest technologies.

The Chinese commune system of collectivized agriculture was also dismantled. The Chinese countryside, known throughout Asia in the decades prior to the 1970s for its egalitarian achievements and social gains for the poorest peasants, became severely stratified again.

While millions of more well-to-do peasants saw a sharp rise in their living standards, a huge mass of rural dwellers lost everything. Left to fend for themselves, they migrated by the tens of millions to urban areas seeking employment in newly created factories—many in special economic zones set aside for foreign capitalist investors. This migrant labor force, uprooted from the land, became the source of human material necessary for the establishment of a new market-based private capitalist sector.

Within 25 years, the People's Republic of China was fully integrated into the capitalist world economy. Foreign direct investment skyrocketed as U.S., European and Japanese capital set up in China to take advantage of the huge labor pool. Transnational corporations helped create the largest industrial work force in the world.

CONTRADICTIONS IN CHINA TODAY

The reforms initiated by the Deng Xiaoping-led government and expanded by subsequent leaderships within the Communist Party of China have given rise to a new bourgeoisie inside China—a class of Chinese with interests opposite those of the Chinese working class, but also distinct from the interests of world imperialism. The CPC-led state has functioned as the protector of this bourgeoisie both in its relations with the Chinese working class and in its relations with the imperialist bourgeoisie.

To the extent that the Chinese state has promoted and enforced the rights, the interests and the needs of the Chinese bourgeoisie and the transnational corporations functioning within China, the state assumes the tasks of a bourgeois state. Since it is a state that originated from a working-class revolution and enjoyed an immense base of support from within the working class and peasantry, the Chinese state has only been able to incrementally, and over a time frame of several decades, diminish its historic obligations to and defense of its original social base.

The Chinese state and the Communist Party of China have essential elements of what is known as Bonapartism. The ruling party has to a degree straddled the class divide and has a foot within both the bourgeoisie and the working class.

The actual living experience of China in its evolution since 1949 is without precedent. Its differences with the Soviet Union's historical experience require us to acknowledge that it is no longer an exactly analogous social formation.

The destruction and incremental dissolution of public ownership, centralized planning and the monopoly of foreign trade constitutes a historic setback for the Chinese working class. Its rights and interests have either been stripped or seriously eroded while the rights of capital, including foreign capital, have been elevated.

The advancement of the Chinese bourgeoisie has been at the expense of the political and social primacy of the working class. To the extent that a larger section of the Chinese population, including the working class, has additional access to goods, it comes as a form of personal or individual acquisition and cannot mask the fact that the status of the working class as a class has been seriously downgraded in terms of its social rights and political weight within the state and party.

The working class and the poor and middle peasants are not equipped as a class to be the link to world capitalism with its needs for super-exploitation on a large scale in China. In fact, the working class and peasantry have antagonistic interests to the needs of capital.

The country of origin for investment capital is completely immaterial to the proletariat. Capital, above all else, is a social relationship between exploiters and exploited. Capital thrives only through exploitation—through the private appropriation and accumulation of surplus value created by collective, living labor. Whether Chinese workers are employed by capitalists from the United States, Germany or Japan, or whether the factory owner is a Chinese capitalist, the relationship is based on exploitation.

Moreover, the class instinct of the Chinese proletariat—no different from any working class—is to resist the demands of globalized international capital and its agents inside of China, who pursue a path of relentless cost-cutting to remain competitive, whether in the world capitalist market, the Asia-wide regional market or in the emerging internal Chinese market.

Cutting wages and social benefits, uprooting working-class neighborhoods for commercial development, and grabbing land in the countryside for capitalist development are typical features of the march of capital. The working class as a class is compelled to resist these incursions, and the phenomenon of class resistance is becoming widespread throughout China.

The economic reforms instituted since 1978 have eviscerated many of the social insurance guarantees previously enjoyed by the workers and even more numerous peasantry. Basic social rights—healthcare coverage for all, the right to a job, free public education, affordable housing—have been severely cut back for millions.

Although it is impossible to say with 100 percent certainty where in this process China is, it is indisputable that the basic trend toward more entrenched capitalist class relations has only deepened since 1978. This process is, however, unfinished. As long as the Communist Party of China retains its hold on political power, there is a possibility, however great or small, that this trend can still be reversed.

The process could also be slowed and stalled in the face of unanticipated developments, such as a global capitalist economic crisis that would likely shake China's export-driven economy to its core, or an internal class or intra-class confrontation—or even a large-scale confrontation with U.S. or Japanese imperialism. It is worth recalling that Yugoslav communists reversed decades of capitalist-oriented economic reforms between 1989 and 1999 in the face of imperialist intervention, dismemberment and internal civil war.

To the extent that workers and peasants in China rebel or resist capitalist encroachments and abuses, they deserve the support of the world working-class movement—especially to the extent that these protests lead toward reversing the gains of capital. The rightful place of the Communist Party of China is with these workers and peasants in their confrontation with the Chinese government and with the domestic and foreign capitalists. When the communists stand aside, they lose credibility with their historic social base.

However, to the extent that these struggles move from spontaneous battles for economic and social justice to movements that are taken over politically by leadership groupings that seek to overthrow the political rule of the Communist Party—as, for instance, occurred with the 1989 Tiananmen Square protests—these struggles can only, under the current political circumstances and absent an organized revolutionary communist leadership current, move into the camp of reactionary counterrevolution. They will be organically connected to and nourished by the forces of world imperialism.

The overthrow of the Communist Party of China in these circumstances would not only lead to the absolute destruction of what is remaining of the old socialist revolution, it would suspend China's bourgeois democratic revolution.

Such an overthrow by non-revolutionary forces would hurl China backward in its epoch-making struggle to emerge from underdevelopment. It would return China to the semi-slavery of comprador neo-colonial rule. China would then also face the possibility of splintering, as happened in Yugoslavia and as may happen in Iraq under the impact of foreign occupation.

In the face of this threat, it is the responsibility of all revolutionaries and progressive people to resist the imperialist offensive and offer militant political defense of the Chinese government—despite profound differences with the theory and practice of so-called "market socialism." ☐

Endnotes

1. "Full text of resolution on amendment to CPC constitution," *People's Daily Online*, October 22, 2007, English.people.com.cn.
2. Frederick Engels, "Draft of a Communist Confession of Faith," written June 9, 1847. Published in *Karl Marx and Frederick Engels Collected Works* vol. 6 (International Publishers, New York, 1976), 96.
3. Frederick Engels, "The Principles of Communism," written in October 1847. Published in *Karl Marx and Frederick Engels Collected Works* vol. 6, 348.
4. See for example, "Market Profile on Chinese Mainland," Hong Kong Trade Development Council, November 7, 2007.
5. Steven R. Weisman, "China Stand on Imports Upsets U.S.," *New York Times*, November 16, 2007.
6. Frederick Engels, "The Principles of Communism," written in October 1847. Published in *Karl Marx and Frederick Engels Collected Works* vol. 6, 351-2.
7. William Hinton, "On the Role of Mao Zedong," *Monthly Review* Volume 56, Number 4, September 2004.
8. For a succinct summary of the Lenin's early view on the centrality of the working class's leadership in Russia's bourgeois democratic revolution, see *A Retrograde Trend in Russian Social-Democracy*, written in 1899, especially pages 270-2 in Lenin's *Collected Works* vol. 4; and the Preface to the Second Edition of *The Development of Capitalism in Russia* (originally written in 1899, second edition in 1907), on pages 31-4 of Lenin's *Collected Works* vol. 3.
9. "Instead of scholastically invented, 'concocted' definitions and fruitless disputes over words (What is socialism? What is communism?), Marx gives an analysis of what might be called the stages of the economic maturity of communism. In its first phase, or first

stage, communism *cannot* as yet be fully mature economically and entirely free from traditions or vestiges of capitalism. Hence the interesting phenomenon that communism in its first phase retains 'the narrow horizon of *bourgeois law*.' Of course, bourgeois law in regard to the distribution of *consumer* goods inevitably presupposes the existence of the *bourgeois state*, for law is nothing without an apparatus capable of *enforcing* the observance of the rules of law. It follows that under communism there remains for a time not only bourgeois law, but even the bourgeois state, without the bourgeoisie!" V.I. Lenin, *State and Revolution*, written in 1917. Published in *Collected Works* vol. 25 (Moscow, Progress Publishers, 1973), 476.

10. Karl Marx, "The Eighteenth Brumaire of Louis Bonaparte," written in 1852. Published in *Karl Marx and Frederick Engels Collected Works* vol. 11, 103.

11. "The state will be able to wither away completely when society adopts the rule: 'From each according to his ability, to each according to his needs,' i.e., when people have become so accustomed to observing the fundamental rules of social intercourse and when their labor has become so productive that they will voluntarily work *according to their ability*. 'The narrow horizon of bourgeois law,' which compels one to calculate with the heartlessness of a Shylock whether one has not worked half an hour more than anybody else, whether one is not getting less pay than somebody else—this narrow horizon will then be left behind." V.I. Lenin, *State and Revolution*, written in 1917. Published in *Collected Works* vol. 25, 474.

12. Maurice Meisner, *The Deng Xiaoping Era: An Inquiry into the Fate of Chinese Socialism, 1978-1994* (New York, Hill and Wang, 1996), 189; Mobo C.F. Gao, *Debating the Cultural Revolution—Do We Only Know What We Believe* (Critical Asian Studies 34, no. 3, September 2002), 424-5.

13. Meisner, *The Deng Xiaoping Era*, 192.

14. Ibid., 193.

CHINA TODAY

Capitalism and socialism in China today

BY ANDY McINERNEY

WRITING in the July/August edition of the Atlantic Monthly, James Fallows, journalist and speechwriter for former President Jimmy Carter, described a recent visit to China. The article, titled "China Makes, the World Takes," is a first-hand view of what is being called the world's factory floor—the Chinese manufacturing industry.

Fallows describes the manufacturing city of Shenzhen, in the southern part of China just north of Hong Kong. The city "did not exist as a city as recently as Ronald Reagan's time in the White House" in the 1980s, with a population of only around 80,000 people—slightly smaller, for example, than Albany, New York.

"Its population has grown at least a hundredfold in the past 25 years," Fallows continues, making it today the size of New York City.

That story—a provincial town booming into an industrial metropolis in just one generation—is the story of China. Fallows' portrait of a modern-day industrial revolution—like Britain in the 19th century or the United States in the 20th—points to the contradictions that have been generated by the market-oriented reforms since 1978.

On the one hand, China today has a modern proletariat. Unlike in 1949, when some 90 percent of the population were peasants, today the majority of Chinese workers are employed in the industrial or service sector.[1] The modern working class is the social basis for socialism.

On the other hand, China's working class has grown in conditions of class contradictions and capitalist exploitation. According to the Chinese government's statistics, 107 million people were either self-employed or worked in privately owned enterprises in 2005.[2] While that is a minority of the total 2005 workforce of 779 million, it is comparable in size to the entire U.S. workforce, which was estimated at 151 million in 2006.[3] These are workers who produce for private profit, either for themselves or for Chinese or foreign capitalists.

The conditions that James Fallows describes are primarily those of workers in this private sector. He describes, for example, the Foxconn works just outside Shenzhen, owned by Taiwanese Terry Guo. Guo is ranked by the 2007 Forbes "World's Billionaires" at the same level as Michael Bloomberg, with assets worth $5.5 billion.

"Some 240,000 people ... work on [Foxconn's] assembly lines, sleep in its dormitories and eat in its company cafeterias. I was told that Foxconn's caterers kill 3,000 pigs each day to feed its employees," Fallows writes.

He describes the normal working conditions for these workers: "A factory shift is typically 12 hours, usually with two breaks for meals (subsidized or free), six or seven days a week. Whenever the action lets up—if the assembly line is down for some reason, if a worker has spare time at a meal break—many people place their heads down on the table in front of them and appear to fall asleep instantly."

The portrait Fallows paints is one that would meet with approval from the leadership of the Communist Party of China. It is the outcome of nearly 30 years of market-oriented economic reforms.

The outcome—a powerful working class on the one hand, intensified exploitation on the other—is the axis for the main contradiction in China today. Two competing economies exist side by side in China: one a remnant of the 1949 socialist revolution, the other having arisen from the introduction of capitalist reforms. How they interact will ultimately impact on the political leadership of the country.

THE LEGACY OF SOCIALISM

With the 1949 revolution, China emerged from centuries of colonialism and feudal backwardness. The historic mission of the bourgeoisie—the development of a nation's productive capacity and the corresponding growth of the modern working class—fell to the working class and its political leadership, the Communist Party of China. In the fierce two-line struggles that took place over the next three decades, all major wings within the CPC understood this historic mission.

In 1975, U.S. sources estimated China's gross domestic product to be $299 billion.[4] That compares to the 1952 GDP of $68 billion in constant dollars; the economy had more than quadrupled.[5] By comparison, the U.S. GDP doubled in the same period.[6]

The tremendous growth rate, despite revolutionary upheavals that took millions of workers out of the farms and factories and into the streets, was based almost entirely on socialist methods of central planning, state-owned industries and communes, and a monopoly on foreign trade.

China launched its first attempt at a five-year plan for the economy in 1953, emphasizing the development of heavy industry. Major industries were socialized by 1955.

The basic unit of economic life in the countryside was the people's commune, introduced with the wholesale collectivization of land in 1958. In 1980, there were 52,000 communes.[7] Based on this centralized organization of agricultural production, China was producing over 260 million tons of grain in 1975, compared to 108 million in 1949.[8]

The emphasis on collective and state forms of property in both the cities and the countryside corresponded to a vast increase of social welfare provisions. In 1983, for example, 96.8 percent of state workers had the right to their job for life. In addition, medical care, housing, child care and pensions were all provided by the state enterprises.[9] More than 75 percent of all workers in the late 1970s had access to free health care, while 90 percent of villages offered some limited health care to rural residents.[10]

THE IMPACT OF REFORMS

Beginning in 1978, the Deng Xiaoping and subsequent Communist Party leaderships began a steady process of dismantling many of the key features of China's socialist economy. The reforms went through a number of phases.[11] From 1978 to 1983, central planning was reduced and market elements were begun to introduce competitive incentives to increase industrial production. Agriculture was decollectivized, with the communes abolished and replaced with "township and village enterprises." Foreign investment was encouraged through the development of "special economic zones" like Shenzhen.

From 1984 to 1991, the Chinese government increased reliance on market mechanisms, including the labor market. Basic workers' rights like guaranteed employment were weakened or abolished outright in order to encourage "labor flexibility." Workers and peasants began to experience features of capitalism such as unemployment and inflation.

Beginning in 1991, the Chinese government put more and more emphasis on private ownership instead of on the state and collective sectors of the economy. In 2001, China joined the World Trade Organization—in return for dropping trade barriers and in effect ending the state's monopoly on foreign trade. "According to the amended Foreign Trade Law which went into effect in July 2004, all types of enterprises, including private enterprises, can register for the trading right. Individual Chinese are also allowed to conduct foreign trade under the amended Foreign Trade Law," reported the Hong Kong Trade Development Council in its Nov. 7, 2007 "Market Profile on the Chinese Mainland."

The reform process has changed China's economic landscape. On the one hand, the Chinese economy has become one of the driving forces of the world capitalist economy. Economic growth has ranged from 7 to 14 percent annually for each year since 1991—compared to 2 to 4 percent annual growth for the U.S. economy. In 2006, China's external trade hit $1.8 trillion,[12] putting it behind only the United States and Germany.

CAPITALISM IN CHINA

The tremendous growth of China's productive capacity as well as its working class has come at the expense of introducing capitalist relations of production into the economy. Much of the capitalist sector is intimately tied to foreign capital from the very countries that kept China chained in neocolonial oppression and exploitation before the revolution.

According to a February 2007 report by the U.S.-China Business Council, foreign direct investment in China stood at 41,485 projects with an actually utilized value of $69 billion. Foreign-invested enterprises account for a disproportionate part of China's exports, making up 58.9 percent of China's expected total trade volume of $2.1 trillion in 2007. That led Morgan Stanley chief economist Stephen Roach to note in October 2006, "The power of the Chinese export machine is mainly an outgrowth of a Western penchant for offshore efficiency solutions"—commonly referred to as outsourcing.

Officially, U.S. corporations and banks make up a relatively small part of China's investment, ranking fifth with less than $3 billion of the $69 billion invested. However, much of the investment income is masked in holding companies registered in third countries. The British Virgin Islands, for example, ranks second with $11 billion—despite the fact that the GDP of the Virgin Islands was not even $1 billion in 2003.

The number of privately owned industrial enterprises has jumped dramatically in the past five years. The 2006 China Statistical Yearbook recorded 10,667 private industrial enterprises in 1998 with an industrial output of 200 billion yuan. That had jumped to 123,820 enterprises with an output of 4.78 trillion yuan by 2005.

The privately-owned and foreign-owned sectors carry inordinate economic weight within the Chinese economy. In addition, the social weight of the 107 million workers employed in these sectors has changed the class dynamics in China.

WHAT REMAINS OF THE STATE ECONOMY

Morgan Stanley chief economist Roach characterized the Chinese economy in 2006: "Despite 27 years of extraordinary reforms, China is still very much a blended economy. Notwithstanding the emergence of a thriving market-based sector, state-owned enterprises still account for about 35 percent of Chinese GDP."

The state-owned enterprises (SOEs) are the main economic remnants of the socialist measures introduced in China from 1952 to 1978. They no longer operate according to a socialist economic plan but are instead being forced to compete against the private and foreign-owned industry on a profit basis.

That said, the country's 159 SOEs yielded $137.5 billion in profits in 2006, according to the Chinese Ministry of Finance in a Jan. 27, 2007 report. The report goes on to note: "The government has been pushing the restructuring and sale of SOEs over the last three years. The number of central SOEs has dropped from 196 to 159 and will be down to around 100 by 2010."

The fact that the SOEs are operating in the semi-public, semi-competitive economic arena has caused some odd social outcomes. A Sept. 26, 2007 article in the Hong Kong-based Asia Times describes the now-profitable SOEs:

The original intention of Beijing's policy to let SOEs keep their profits was for them to expand their businesses. However, nearly all of them have used the staggering profits to benefit their management and employees. Salaries of managers and employees in SOEs in state monopolized industries are much higher than the average. They are also often given handsome cash bonuses. Many of the enterprises also used company funds to build housing for their employees, and equipping even the lowest-ranking officials with cars.

This results in unfairness and injustice in social wealth redistribution, which increasingly angers the public. Many people have rightly complained that since the SOEs are supposed[ly] owned by all people, their profits must be shared by all people, instead of by such a minority of persons working within them.

To the extent that economic planning still occurs, it is carried out by the National Development and Reform Commission, which is responsible for drawing up and overseeing the country's five-year plans. Well-known economist and China expert Gregory Chow of Princeton summarized the basic character of the NDRC's predecessor in 2004: "Much of the administrative process for plan formulation before 1978 is applicable today. Only the content of the plan is different. In a market economy, much of productive and distributive activities are no longer included in the plan."[13]

The methods of central government control, Chow notes, is based on "control of money supply, the interest rate and the foreign exchange rate"—that is, using the same elements of state planning used by the U.S. Federal Reserve, for example. Planning encompasses the private sector activity. "By allowing or even fostering the market sector to compete with government enterprises which are held financially accountable," Chow writes, "the line between suitable government and market activities is naturally drawn."[14]

In short, China retains the shell of a centrally planned economy. How well the growing private sector will fit into the shell will depend on the class struggle inside China and the fate of the world capitalist market on which the Chinese economy now depends.

It should be noted, though, that the combined elements of state planning, the protection of national capital and the continued existence of a state industrial sector have prevented China from experiencing a recession or depression—characterized by the destruction of productive capital or negative GDP growth—since 1978. Recessions are a basic feature of capitalism. The United States has experienced four since 1978, roughly every 10 years.

Today, it is virtually inconceivable that a world economic crisis would not impact China. When the export sector of the Chinese economy is entirely oriented toward the capitalist market, a downturn in the United States or the rest of the capitalist world would immediately reverberate in China, with factory shutdowns and layoffs.

THE SITUATION FACING CHINESE WORKERS

China's rapid economic development has led to dramatic improvements in access to goods, especially in larger urban areas but also throughout the country. However, there has also been a dramatic increase in inequality, especially in access to health care, education, wages and other measures of social insurance.

China's Gini index,[15] an international statistic that measures income inequality, has grown from 44.5 in 1995 to 46.5 in 2004. In 2005, it jumped again to 47. By this measure, income inequality in China has become worse than in the United States, whose Gini index in 2004 was 45.

An official 2006 Chinese government document titled "Report of the Development of an Overall Well-off Society" stated that 48 million Chinese lived below the government-acknowledged poverty line—26 million in the countryside and the rest in the cities. An additional 87 million fall under the internationally recognized poverty line—a total of 10 percent of the population.

During the early period of the economic reforms that began in 1978, health care coverage provided by state-sponsored programs existed in 90 percent of China's villages. By the 1990s, that coverage had fallen to less than 5 percent.[16] As a result, the majority of the population no longer has access to free or heavily subsidized health care.[17]

When they were employed at state-owned factories prior to the economic reforms, the vast majority of industrial workers were guaranteed lifetime employment, health care insurance and pensions.

By 2002, more than 24 million workers had been laid off from these enterprises as they were transformed into privately owned capitalist companies.[18]

The economic status of China's migrant workers, many of whom left the rural villages after the dismantling of the communes, is perilous. Of the 140 million migrant workers in 2007, only 27 million were eligible to receive benefits if they lost employment because of job-related injuries.[19]

Class struggles of all sorts are raging in China today. With the largest industrial wage-earning workforce in the world being exploited by foreign and domestic capitalists, the dislocation of peasants from the land, and the opening up of private and semi-public real-estate acquisitions on land that had been collectively or state owned, it is natural that there are thousands of job actions and protests throughout the country.

> To satisfy the demands of international capital, the government has compromised the institutional rights of the Chinese workers and peasants.

The current Communist Party leadership is well aware of the danger of social unrest and its potential impact on its continued hold on political power.

To satisfy the demands of international capital, the government has compromised the institutional rights of the Chinese workers and peasants. Now it is taking measures to create some balance and some additional limits on the nearly unfettered rights of the transnational corporations.

In June 2007, China's National People's Congress adopted a labor reform bill over the objection of the international capitalists requiring employers to provide workers with written contracts including long-term job security provisions. In addition, the bill, scheduled to become law in 2008, restricts the use of temporary laborers by the companies.[20] The law also strengthens the hand of the official communist-led national trade union in negotiating over wages and benefits.[21]

In August 2006, after intense negotiations with the Chinese government to enter China, Wal-Mart announced that it would agree to allow the All-China Federation of Trade Unions to represent Wal-Mart workers in China. "After overcoming stiff resistance from Wal-Mart, which has long fought to bar unions from its stores and distribution centers, the official [ACFTU] now plans to focus on other companies in China." (International Herald Tribune, Oct. 12, 2006)

In April 2007, McDonalds recognized the ACFTU at its 750 outlets. The ACFTU announced that it was aiming to organize 70 percent of foreign-invested companies by 2008. (New York Times, April 10, 2007)

The government also submitted legislation in June 2007 that would provide some semblance of pension rights for China's 140 million migrant workers. This legislation is not a guaranteed state-sponsored pension program but rather established a mechanism for employers and employees to pay into a pension fund that a migrant worker takes from one job to the next.[22]

THE ROLE OF THE CPC

The role of a revolutionary communist party is to lead the workers and peasants in their struggle against exploitation and those who oppress them. That was the historic role of the Communist Party of China.

Today, however, the CPC is in many ways a hybrid. At its inception in 1921 and for the next eight decades, the Communist Party of China described itself as the vanguard of the working class and poor peasantry. Some of the same language is still employed today.

At the same time, the CPC is managing a government that has turned away from the socialist economic road in favor of integration into a world economy entirely dominated by capitalist banks and corporations.

This has turned the CPC itself into an arena of class struggle. The struggle over which class will rule, the capitalists or the workers, is being played out in party congresses at every level.

The new pro-labor reforms are a reflection of this contradictory class orientation. They are aimed at making concessions to the workers and poor. But for the pro-capitalist elements within the CPC, the goal of the new reforms is to blunt the class struggle so that it does not get out of control. This is more akin to the role of the classic social democratic parties when they took the helm of capitalist governments in Europe and Japan.

Of course, classic western social democracy with its attendant social contract with labor was premised on wealth accumulated through the process of looting colonies and semi-colonies. China has not had that history of plunder and looting; on the contrary, it has historically been on the receiving end.

The paradox facing the CPC is that its historic working-class base will inevitably be drawn into struggle against the capitalist economic forces. Their target will include the CPC-led government, which has given capitalists, foreign and domestic, permission and encouragement to thrive inside China.

Sectors within the Chinese capitalist class, especially those most closely tied to imperialist interests, will also seek to loosen the CPC's grip on the government and over the economy. For the world imperialist powers that see in China both vast markets and labor as well as a potentially powerful rival, the CPC represents an obstacle to their interests.

This is a historically unstable political situation. This fundamental contradiction will play out amid a growing world economic contraction. It will play out in the face of western-backed counterrevolution that will exploit the justified grievances of the working class. How the contradiction is resolved will determine the fate of China, its people, and the global balance of class forces for decades to come. □

Endnotes

1. *2007 CIA World Factbook.* See also 2006 China Statistical Yearbook.
2. "Number of Persons in Private Enterprises and Self-employed Individuals at the Year-end by Sector and Region," Table 5-13, 2006 *China Statistical Yearbook.*
3. *2007 CIA World Factbook.*
4. C. MacDougall, "The Chinese Economy in 1976," *China Quarterly* 70 (June 1977), 360.
5. Joint SSBC—Hitotsubashi University Team, "The Historical Accounts of the People's Republic of China, 1952–1995," September 1997.
6. Louis D. Johnston and Samuel H. Williamson, "The Annual Real and Nominal GDP for the United States, 1790 - Present." *Economic History Services,* October 2005.
7. J Domes, "New Policies in the Communes," *Journal of Asian Studies* vol. 41 no. 2 (February 1982), 253.
8. V. Lippit, "The Commune in Chinese Development," *Modern China* vol. 3 no. 2 (April 1977), 254-55.

9. G. White, "The Politics of Economic Reform in Chinese Industry," *China Quarterly* no. 111 (September 1987), 366.

10. Zh. Zhao, "Income Inequality, Unequal Health Care Access and Mortality in China," *Population and Development Review* vol. 32 no. 3 (September 2006), 473.

11. See M Hart-Landsberg and P. Burkett, "China and Socialism: Market Reforms and Class Struggle," *Monthly Review,* (July-August 2004), 31-50.

12. "Market Profile on the Chinese Mainland," *Hong Kong Trade Development Council,* Nov. 7, 2007.

13. G. C. Chow, "The Role of Planning in China's Market Economy," paper presented at the International Conference on China's Planning System Reform, Beijing, March 24-25, 2004, sponsored by China's State Development and Reform Commission, State Law Office and the Asian Development Bank.

14. Ibid.

15. According to the Gini index scale, 0 represents perfect equality (every family earning the same amount) where 100 represents perfect inequality (one family owns all the wealth and the rest of families own none). According to the CIA World Factbook, Gini indices range from the mid-20s for Scandinavian countries to the 50s and 60s for countries in Latin America and Africa.

16. *Income Inequality, Unequal Health Care Access, and Mortality in China,* 461.

17. Ibid., 462

18. Jasper Becker, *Christian Science Monitor,* October 21, 2002.

19. *People's Daily Online,* June 11, 2007.

20. Joseph Kahn and David Barboza *The New York Times,* June 30, 2007.

21. Ibid.

22. *Peoples Daily Online,* June 11, 2007.

Is China's appeasement policy sustainable?

BY GLORIA LA RIVA

THE foreign policy of the People's Republic of China is complex, but the central axis is China's relationship with U.S. imperialism. Since the 1970s, the Chinese government has pursued a nationalist rather than a proletarian internationalist line and program. The number one goal of the leadership is for China to go from being an "underdeveloped" country to a "medium-level developed country" by around 2050—a formulation used by China Reform Forum Chair Zheng Bijian in a Dec. 9, 2005 speech titled "Ten Views on China's Development Road of Peaceful Rise."[1]

For this to happen, the Communist Party of China leadership believes, Chinese foreign policy must appease the United States. It must recognize U.S. imperialism's vital global interests, particularly in regard to the Middle East. Should it fail to do so, it risks becoming the target of U.S. aggression.

For that reason, even though China had important relations with Iraq and has close ties to Iran and other states in the region, it has done everything possible to minimize conflict with Washington. In key United Nations votes, China at various times abstained or voted for the sanctions against Iraq in the 1990s and against Iran in 2006 and 2007.

Aside from the fact that the internationalist and communist obligation is to stand with oppressed nations against imperialism, these moves appear to sacrifice even China's narrow national interests. They harm its key allies and strengthen the hand of an imperialist power that is clearly still antagonistic.

China's foreign policy is based on a clear identification of its own economic development as the top priority. To this end, China must avoid open conflict with the United States and be engaged with rather than isolated from the forces of capitalist economic globalization, according to the central logic of its highly nuanced foreign policy.

Despite all efforts to avoid conflict and the opening of China's economy to massive foreign capitalist investment, the U.S. ruling class's fundamental hostility toward China has not been diminished. Its aim is to weaken and ultimately end the CPC's control of the state, completely open up the economy and end the possibility of China emerging as a power that might one day challenge U.S. global supremacy.

PHASES OF U.S.-CHINA RELATIONS

For over two decades following the 1949 Chinese Revolution, U.S. policy toward China was one of war, embargo and intense hostility. Washington had backed Chiang Kai-shek's defeated reactionary Nationalist Party (Kuomintang, or KMT) government to the tune of billions of dollars. In the United States, the victory of the Chinese Revolution set off a new round of anti-communist purges led by Sen. Joseph McCarthy.

Just one year after the 1949 revolution, 1 million members of the Chinese People's Volunteer Army crossed into Korea to defend the revolution there against the massive U.S.-U.N. invasion of the Korean peninsula. Although there had scarcely been time for the Chinese people to begin rebuilding their famished and war-torn country, internationalist principles of working class solidarity guided China's support for Korea. China's intervention was decisive in forcing the United States to accept a 1953 armistice.

China suffered hundreds of thousands of casualties in defending Korea. Among those killed in battle was Mao Anying, CPC leader Mao Zedong's son.

In 1950, China and the Soviet Union signed a treaty of mutual aid and defense. Over the next decade, the Soviets extended crucial economic and technical aid to China. This period saw the emergence of the "socialist camp"—a bloc of countries building socialism in Europe and Asia that together encompassed at least two-fifths of humanity.

In the early 1960s, the CPC issued a series of polemics criticizing the Soviet leadership for prioritizing "peaceful coexistence" with U.S. imperialism over support for revolutionary movements. They also criticized Communist Party of the Soviet Union first secretary Nikita Khrushchev's idea that socialism could be achieved by non-revolutionary means. Together, these critiques invigorated new revolutionary forces who were disillusioned with the Soviet leadership's reformist line.

Khrushchev responded to the critiques by cutting off all aid to China.

During this entire period, U.S. hostility toward China was unrelenting. The U.S. Seventh Fleet was based off Japan's and South Korea's coasts, very close to China. The massive U.S. invasion of Vietnam was widely understood to be directed against China as well. The U.S. government forbade any U.S. company to trade with China. Washington blocked the world's most populous country from entering the United Nations, maintaining the bizarre fiction that the regime of corrupt and defeated Chiang Kai-shek was the true representative of the Chinese people.

By the late 1960s, CPC leaders began calling the Soviet Union "social imperialist" and "fascist." The growing hostility between the former allies was cheered within U.S. ruling circles. For both liberal and conservative wings, fostering divisions between the two socialist countries became a political priority.

Still, it was a shock to the international communist movement and all those struggling against imperialism when China and the United States entered into a strategic alliance in the early 1970s. The new alliance was directed primarily against the Soviet Union, but also against other states in the socialist bloc and national liberation movements that sided with the Soviet Union and its allies.

U.S.-CHINA ALLIANCE

China explained its foreign policy publicly as pushing back the "hegemony" of Soviet "social-imperialism," which it now called the "greatest danger" to the people of the world.

Putting aside for a moment its false characterization that the Soviet Union was imperialist, China's main motivation in its overtures to U.S. imperialism was to garner a major economic and political relationship with the United States. It also sought to win recognition of the "one–China principle," ending the official U.S. recognition of the bourgeois regime in Taiwan.

In 1971, following a round of secret diplomacy that resulted in U.S. president Richard Nixon visiting China the next year, the United States dropped its opposition and China entered the United Nations. The U.S. embargo had been ended earlier that year and formal diplomatic relations were established by the end of the 1970s.

Once the Chinese leadership made a definite turn toward the United States in 1971, U.S. rulers felt freer to pursue a more aggressive line against the Soviet Union, its socialist allies and revolutionary movements worldwide. The first steps were taken while Mao Zedong was still China's preeminent leader. But the U.S.-China alliance reached its fullest expression under the government of Deng Xiaoping.

China aligned itself with U.S. counterrevolutionary interventions worldwide in the 1970s and 1980s. The Chinese government supported the fascist Pinochet regime in Chile.

In Africa, revolutions successfully overthrew the colonial Portuguese rulers in Angola, Mozambique, Guinea-Bissau, São Tomé and Príncipe, and Cape Verde in 1975 following a revolution in Portugal. Ethiopia's emperor, Haile Selassie, was overthrown in 1974, and revolutionaries struggled to build socialism. In all these cases, the Pentagon armed, trained and financed counterrevolutionaries from the Horn of Africa to the former Portuguese colonies, inflicting grave damage on the newly liberated states and costing millions of lives.

Consistent with the rest of its new foreign policy, China also supplied arms to the counterrevolutionary National Union for the Total Independence of Angola (UNITA) and National Front for the Liberation of Angola (FNLA) in Angola and to reactionaries fighting to dismember Ethiopia.

CHINA INVADES VIETNAM

In 1979, Chinese troops invaded Vietnam. Just prior to the invasion, Chinese deputy prime minister Deng Xiaoping visited Washington for talks with President Jimmy Carter. Undoubtedly, China's plans against Vietnam were a subject of discussions in Washington, given China's deepening alliance with the United States.

Before his arrival, Deng was interviewed by Time magazine. "The question is: After setting up this relationship between China, Japan and the United States, we must further develop the relationship in a deepening way," Deng said. "If we really want to be able to place curbs on the polar bear, the only realistic thing for us is to unite. If we only depend on the strength of the U.S., it is not enough. If we only depend on the strength of Europe, it is not enough. We are an insignificant, poor country, but if we unite, well, it will then carry weight. ... We consider that the true hotbed of war is the Soviet Union, not the U.S."[2]

This claim flew in the face of the fact that the U.S. government was pumping billions of dollars in military spending to reverse the revolutions in Angola, Mozambique, Ethiopia, Nicaragua and Afghanistan.

Deng made China's announcement of a pending invasion of Vietnam on the first day possible following the expiration of the 1950 Sino-Soviet peace treaty.

Two days later, on Feb. 17, 1979, China invaded Vietnam with some 100,000 troops. Progressives around the world condemned that action. Vietnam's fierce resistance defeated the Chinese forces, which finally withdrew after three weeks.

AN EPHEMERAL ALLIANCE

Bourgeois political pundits in every U.S. administration from Nixon to Reagan would periodically raise alarms over the possibility of détente between the Soviet Union and China. This was a development to be avoided at all costs. The class-conscious U.S. ruling class knew that a renewal of a Sino-Soviet alliance would be a huge setback to their aim of global domination. Despite sharp political differences, there was no objective basis for disputes between the two workers' states.

In the late 1980s and early 1990s, the Soviet Union was in the throes of counterrevolution. Washington's need for an alliance with China against what had been the bulwark of the socialist camp was coming to an end.

China's belief that its alliance with U.S. imperialism was on firm ground proved to be illusory. The real winners from the U.S.-China alliance were the United States and its imperialist allies.

The alliance only lasted as long as it was advantageous for the United States, no matter what China wished for or how strongly it embraced U.S. foreign policy.

Even during their closest collaboration, Washington still maintained Taiwan as an armed fortress against the People's Republic of China.

U.S. imperialism never lost sight of the fact that China was still a socialist state. In 1989, U.S. imperialism turned on China, throwing its weight behind the Tiananmen Square student demonstrations—a not-so-hidden attempt to overthrow the Chinese state.

After repeated attempts at a peaceful resolution, China's army was forced to break up the student demonstrations, which had become increasingly violent and whose leadership was supported by—if not under the direction of—the CIA. Hundreds of people died in the showdown on June 4, 1989—half or more of them government soldiers and police.

The U.S. media launched a fierce attack after China suppressed the counterrevolutionary attempt, wildly claiming that "tens of thousands" of students had been massacred.

The Tiananmen Square events marked the end of the U.S.-China alliance.

CHINA'S POLICY IN A UNIPOLAR WORLD

Since the collapse of its anti-Soviet alliance with U.S. imperialism, China's foreign policy has veered between borderline subservience to U.S. imperialism and a genuine independent world orientation.

China's growing economic power in the world economy makes it impossible for U.S. imperialism to approach China as a complete vassal. A huge part of the consumer goods sold in the United States by U.S. and foreign corporations are manufactured in China. These economic relations have continued to expand, despite the end of the strategic political alliance.

It is estimated, for example, that China's National Bank now holds $1.4 trillion in foreign reserves, mainly in U.S. dollars. This gives China a powerful influence over the U.S. economy. The large Chinese purchases of U.S. treasury bonds, for example, is a factor allowing the U.S. Federal Reserve to keep interest rates low. This increases the ability of corporations to expand their production and for consumers to buy with credit.

In addition, China is developing deeper economic and political ties with countries considered enemy states by U.S. imperialism, like Iran, Venezuela and Cuba. The pacts have been helpful to those countries and others as well, aiding both economic development and providing the possibility of an alliance with China that will give the anti-imperialist countries breathing space.

The U.S. rulers, dedicated as they are to the strategy of maintaining a unipolar world, view China as a—perhaps the—long-term threat to U.S. hegemony. Economic, political and other interests aside, the ultimate aim of the U.S. government's China policy remains regime change and the destruction of China as a potential challenger to U.S. global domination.

This objective contradiction between U.S. imperialism and Chinese development will be the biggest obstacle to China's "peaceful rise," despite the Chinese government's best efforts at conciliation and accommodation. ☐

Endnotes

1. Speech given on behalf of the China Reform Forum, Zheng Bijian, "Ten Views on China's Development Road of Peaceful Rise and Sino European Relations," December 9, 2005, http://www.chinaembassy.nl/eng/xwdt/t232099.htm.
2. "An Interview with Teng Hsiao-p'ing [Deng Xiaoping]," *Time*, February 5, 1979.

Chinese economic aid

Independent development versus imperialist domination

BY CANEISHA MILLS

O N May 14, 2007, Nigeria successfully placed into orbit its first telecommunications satellite. Nigerian television carried a live broadcast of the launch, and the country's newspapers proudly declared that the event represented a historic turning point in the effort to modernize and diversify Nigeria's oil-driven economy.

Nigeria's first satellite launch was the result of an agreement between Nigeria and the People's Republic of China. Chinese engineers designed and built the satellite. It was launched from Sichuan province in China. When imperialist banks and corporations refused to provide loans to cover the costs estimated at $300 million, a state-owned bank in China provided about $200 million in preferential buying credits.

Launching this satellite will "revolutionize telecommunications, broadcasting and broadband multimedia services in Africa," according to the May 14, 2007, Hindustan Times. It is expected to create over 150,000 new jobs and bring the Internet to once remote locations throughout the country.

This technological advancement is a beacon of hope for Nigeria and all of Africa. It gives a clue of what is possible. It gives hope to millions across the continent—in some ways reminiscent of the Soviet Union's 1957 launch of Sputnik, the first space satellite.

The perception in wide sectors of Africa—grounded in centuries of colonial exploitation and oppression—is that western capitalist corporations only seek to invest in Africa to extract and exploit its vast natural resources. The Angolans, Sudanese, Zimbabweans and other formerly colonized people of Africa have not forgotten the "legacy of western development." It was development based on the pillage and plunder of natural resources and the slaughter of African people.

Underdevelopment in Africa and all over the world is the legacy of centuries of colonial and neocolonial domination over oppressed countries. Imperialist powers continue today to vie for access to markets and labor in these countries. It is the basis for the corporations and banks to extract what V.I. Lenin called "super-profits"—profits above and beyond the "normal" rate of profit in the imperialist homelands.

But the Chinese-Nigerian satellite launch is evidence that there is a new global economic powerhouse that is willing to lend assistance to the formerly colonized and semi-colonized countries to modernize and develop their national economies in exchange for access to natural resources.

China, like Nigeria, is a country that was also left on its knees by the cruel legacy of colonialism and imperialist-induced economic underdevelopment. Its economic growth is a powerful indicator of the profound and lasting impact caused by the victorious Chinese Revolution of 1949.

Just 20 years ago, the main goal of the Chinese government was to create an economic plan that would meet the most basic needs of its own people. To reach this goal, China needed to more than triple its current gross domestic product. By March 2001, the Chinese government proudly proclaimed they had exceeded their expectations. The Chinese GDP was $1.77 trillion. Today China has one of the fastest-growing economies in the world.

Growth of the Chinese economy has been directly paralleled by its increasing investment and economic aid in Africa. Nigeria is just one example.

DEVELOPMENT IN AFRICA ...

Since the collapse of the Soviet Union, the United States and other imperialist powers have thrown down a challenge to oppressed countries: The only hope for development is to subordinate your economies and your politics to the needs of imperialism. China is now providing a space to anti-imperialist governments and to those countries that are trying to get better economic terms than those dictated by the United States or the International Monetary Fund. This fills the gap for governments that are isolated by imperialism.

The majority of Chinese oil imports come from Angola, a country still suffering the effects of a U.S.-funded counterrevolutionary war that took place throughout the 1970s and 1980s. In May 2006, Angola and China signed an agreement to develop another oil field. Several other projects based on economic credit from China will also help repair the transportation industry in Angola. These multi-billion-dollar agreements will revolutionize the roads, airports and administrative buildings throughout the country.

Like Nigeria, Angola could not complete many of these programs without foreign investment. Unlike loans from the International Monetary Fund, Chinese economic agreements come with fewer restrictions and qualifiers.

Currently, China is the largest investor in Zimbabwe—where U.S. and British imperialists are trying to force the government out of power. In the first six months of 2007, trade between the two countries reached a total of $205 million. Chinese investments have increased the number of passenger planes for Air Zimbabwe, fighter jets for the country's air force, and buses for public transportation.

Sudan is another African country in the crosshairs of the imperialists. Its largest trading partner is also China. Awad Ahmed Al-Jaz, minister of energy and mining of Sudan commented on the economic growth of the country: "Thanks to the CNPC's [China National Petroleum Corporation] strong assistance, Sudan has transformed itself from a crude-oil-importing country into a crude-oil-exporting country. ... Sudan's overall economy is developing vigorously and entering a phase of economic boom."

... AND LATIN AMERICA

In Latin America, Cuba and Venezuela form a new axis for anti-imperialist cooperation. China is providing essential support.

Venezuela is a primary example. In 1999, when Chávez was elected president, Venezuela sold no oil to China. Today, Venezuela exports 300,000 barrels per day to China. This number is scheduled to expand and is projected to reach 1 million barrels per day by 2010.

China has also provided $4 billion to finance joint projects that include the manufacture of cellular phones, automobiles and railroads. Through its relations with China, Venezuela has been able to loosen the grip of U.S. imperialism on its economy.

According to various reports, "China has solidified its position as Cuba's second-ranked commercial partner and trade will continue to increase." At the China-Venezuela 14th Intergovernmental Commission for Economic and Commercial Relations meeting, the two countries' representatives stressed the need for increased investment in biotechnology. They also highlighted their accomplishments based on joint projects with China.

China restarted a nickel processing plant in Cuba with a $500 million investment. Cubaniquel, Cuba's state entity, owns 51 percent of the operation and Minmetals of China, also state-owned, owns 49 percent.

Cuba's transportation system, in dire need of repair and revitalization, deteriorated due to the U.S. blockade and collapse of trade with the Soviet Union. In 2006 and 2007, China sold 100 locomotives to Cuba, and several thousand new buses for the island's inter- and intra-city transport.

China is financing a $70 million project between the revolutionary governments of Cuba and Venezuela to construct an underwater fiber-optics cable to Cuba to enable Internet communications. It is also engaged with Venezuela in a number of economic deals that could help ensure oil and energy supplies to China.

Despite the fact that it is pursuing its own national economic motivation for those ties, China's trade pacts are an objective challenge to Washington's attempts to strangle and destabilize Cuba and Venezuela.

CHINA IS NOT PART OF THE IMPERIALIST CLUB

China's growth as an emerging industrial power is portrayed in the corporate media, and by some on the left, as proof of a new economic super-power. The imagery of the characterization suggests that China has emerged as a new imperialist power desiring to exploit Africa, Latin America, the Middle East and Asia.

This is a false picture and should be understood as an effort to demonize China by the real imperialist powers in the world. China is still ranked as an underdeveloped country. Its leaders explicitly state that their goal is for China to become a medium-developed country by 2050.

Imperialism, as understood by Marxists, is the emergence of capitalism into its monopoly stage. This process was completed by the start of the 20th century. A handful of industrially advanced capitalist powers in western Europe, the United States and Japan gained control over the whole world in a feverish competition for markets and spheres of influence that allowed for the export of surplus capital. Finance capital or megabanks located in these capitalist countries became the dominant economic power overseeing the partition of the world.

China and the rest of Asia, Africa, Latin America and the Middle East were plundered and colonized or were the victims of semi-colonization.

Their land, labor and resources were stolen leading to the enrichment of the imperialists and the impoverishment and under-development of the colonies. This process is brilliantly explained by Guyanese Marxist Walter Rodney in his classic work "How Europe Underdeveloped Africa."

There are countless examples that prove that China's international investments are not promoting underdevelopment but helping to overcome underdevelopment.

V.I. Lenin, the Marxist leader of the Russian Revolution explained in his book "Imperialism: the Highest Stage of Capitalism": "Monopoly has grown out of colonial policy. To the numerous 'old' motives of colonial policy, finance capital has added the struggle for the sources of raw materials, for the export of capital, for spheres of influence, i.e., for spheres for profitable deals, concessions, monopoly profits and so on, economic territory in general. When the colonies of the European powers, for instance, comprised only one-tenth of the territory of Africa (as was the case in 1876), colonial policy was able to develop—by methods other than those of monopoly—by the 'free grabbing' of territories, so to speak. But when nine-tenths of Africa had been seized (by 1900), when the whole world had been divided up, there was inevitably ushered in the era of monopoly possession of colonies and, consequently, of particularly intense struggle for the division and the re-division of the world."

Imperialist competition for the domination and control of colonies has led to two world wars and innumerable smaller wars.

China was made poor and victimized by imperialism. It rises today not from the plundering but rather from the plundered part of the world. It is still on the receiving end of imported capital from the imperialist transnational corporations. It seeks raw materials and natural resources to emerge from the cruel legacy of underdevelopment. Its exports do not enslave and make colonies out of the importing countries. In fact, there are countless examples that prove that China's international investments are not promoting underdevelopment but helping to overcome underdevelopment. The fact that China's leaders do not promote revolutionary internationalism as a policy, as they did in the 1960s, does not in any way prove that their economic efforts to secure access to raw materials and markets function under the same mechanism as imperialist exploitation. And their political and economic relationship with Cuba, Venezuela, Sudan, and other countries in the so-called "Third World" is empirical proof that China's role in the world is, in fact, a counter-point to rather than an extension of imperialist domination. □

From toy recalls to the Olympics

Behind the U.S. smears against China

BY NATHALIE HRIZI

C HINA is in the U.S. media's spotlight almost all the time. With some notable exceptions, few of the stories seek to provide a greater understanding of China's people, government or economy. Instead, they aim to show how bad things are in the most populous country on earth.

Although there is a great deal of cooperation between the Chinese government and both the U.S. government and transnational corporations, deeper antagonisms with China are never far from the surface. The media campaign against China is rooted in opposition to China's ruling Communist Party and its independent social and economic path. The ongoing antagonism also springs from the fact that Chinese goods compete with U.S. goods in the world market.

On top of the big-business attacks against China, the leaderships of the union federations like the AFL-CIO and Change to Win also take part in the China-bashing campaigns. Weakened by the anti-labor assault by the corporate bosses and facing the intractable problem of job outsourcing, sectors of the U.S. labor bureaucracy have resorted to demagogic attacks against China.

This campaign dovetails with racism and xenophobia, encouraging narrow protectionist policies that divide workers along national lines rather than build labor solidarity. Instead of adopting a class-wide, militant movement to defend the U.S. working class, these "leaders" seek to make common cause with the corporations and convince them to stop doing business in China. Rather than effectively fight the bosses, these union officials resort to scapegoating China.

The corporate-owned media operate as mouthpieces for different sectors of ruling class opinion. They have no love for the labor movement; they are more than willing to promote labor leaders who will stand side-by-side with corporate executives in their anti-China crusade. Of course, there is no shortage of China-bashing allies in the U.S. government as well, Democrats and Republicans alike.

Two major sources of anti-China stories have been the recall of toys exported from China by the Mattel Corp. and the 2008 Beijing Olympics.

Whatever the alleged causes—the supposed quality of export goods, China's supposed support for "genocide" in Africa, its supposed "suppression" of the Dalai Lama's theocracy or its supposed threats to "democracy" in Hong Kong—the goal is the same: to whip up working-class people's anger against the People's Republic of China.

TOY RECALLS

California-based toy maker Mattel, Inc. recalled 20 million Chinese-manufactured toys on Aug. 14, 2007. This was Mattel's second recall that summer. The first was of 1.5 million Fisher-Price toys.

Ruling-class reactions to the recalls were blustery and indignant. Newspaper headlines warned parents away from buying toys made in China.

Mattel's Chairman and CEO Robert Eckert initially blamed China for the recalls. Canadian, U.S. and European capitalist politicians threatened action if China's government did not improve product safety immediately.

In July, two U.S. senators proposed legislation banning Chinese-made products without safety certification. In August, Democratic senator Dick Durbin said, "We can't wait any longer for China to crack down on its lax safety standards. This needs to stop now before more children and more families are put at risk."

The reality of the situation, however, is very different from its portrayal in the capitalist press.

Toy recalls are not unusual. In fact, product recalls in general are not that unusual. The same day that Mattel announced its recall, Nokia recalled 46 million batteries installed in its cell phones. In August 2006, Dell recalled over 4 million batteries installed in its notebook computers.

According to a September 2007 article published by the Asian Pacific Foundation of Canada, the first instance of a toy recall recorded by the U.S. Consumer Product Safety Commission was in 1974. Since that time, 680 toys have been recalled, the majority in the last 20 years.

Recalls originate in either design or manufacturing flaws. The same APFC article points out that, of the 550 recalls since 1988, 76.4 percent were due to design flaws as opposed to manufacturing flaws. Design flaws are directly attributable to the toy corporation, not the country in which the toy is manufactured.

The great majority of the Mattel toys recalled in August were taken off the shelves due to a design flaw—a flaw with absolutely no correlation to where they were produced.

Mattel was forced to admit this on Sept. 21, 2007. The corporation issued an apology to the Chinese people, also admitting that it was "overly inclusive" with its recalls and many of the toys recalled were not a risk at all.

Furthermore, Mattel actually owns the plants that produce its most popular toys. Starting in the late 1980s, Mattel moved toward owning and operating its plants in countries like China, rather than subcontracting. About 50 percent of the company's revenue comes from products made in company-run factories.

Recalls stemming from lead paint have been increasing. Of the 54 toy recalls due to manufacturing flaws in the last 20 years, 31 were due to lead paint. About half were toys made in China; the remainder were made in Australia, Hong Kong (while still under British colonial rule), India, South Korea, Mexico and Taiwan (a virtual U.S. garrison state, despite the fact that it is historically part of China).

The intended effect of the massive anti-China propaganda has been to build an image of China as a monolithic manufacturing colossus that cares only about cutting costs, and not human safety.

In a poll conducted by Canada's Embassy magazine, 75 percent of respondents had an unfavorable view of Chinese-made goods. According to a Zogby poll, nearly 80 percent were apprehensive about buying Chinese-made goods; 63 percent said that they were likely to join a boycott, if called, until the Chinese government improved its regulation of manufacturers. The capitalist-directed vilification of China has certainly been effective.

The attacks on China are not based on the ruling class's concern for children or product safety. American capitalists like the fact that

China exports toys at low cost to them and has made reforms that have opened up a cheap labor market.

China has become a center for the world's toy-making industry, exporting $7.5 billion worth of toys last year and accounting for nearly 87 percent of the toys imported by the United States, according to China's Commerce Ministry.

But the imperialists do not want to compete with China, nor do they want it to surpass them in economic growth or dominance. The imperialists ultimately want to completely gut the remaining socialist vestiges of China's revolution and reopen China to unfettered imperialist exploitation. Weakening China's influence and image is a key component of this campaign.

It is not surprising that the major organizations responsible for generating information about China's factory and manufacturing conditions are on the U.S. government's payroll. China Labor Watch and the China Labour Bulletin are financed by the CIA-connected National Endowment for Democracy.

The group Students and Scholars Against Corporate Misbehavior, which often originates the critiques of Chinese manufacturing, is connected with AFL-CIO's Solidarity Center. The Solidarity Center has supported numerous reactionary movements around the world under the cover of official union affiliation. Around 75 percent of its budget comes from U.S. government funds.

CAMPAIGN AGAINST BEIJING OLYMPICS

The 2008 Beijing Olympics also are being used as an opportunity to berate the Chinese government and its people. The campaign is part of the general anti-China offensive, although this one targets China's developing role in Africa, one of the most resource-rich parts of the globe.

The U.S. propaganda machine has fully mobilized to cast a negative light on China.

U.S. lawmakers have introduced three separate bills calling for a boycott of the Beijing Olympics. The pretext: China's economic partnership and support for the government of Sudan.

According to these legislators as well as the "Save Darfur" campaign and celebrity supporters like Mia Farrow and George Clooney, Chinese support for Sudan has given international cover to "genocide" in Darfur. Farrow refers to the Beijing games as the "Genocide Olympics."

The "Save Darfur" alliance, which calls for a western "humanitarian" intervention in Darfur, has become a pillar in this developing campaign against China. Its website features an action item called, "China and Sudan: Deadly Partnership," which marries anti-Arab imagery and racism with Cold War anti-communism. The complex political and economic crisis in the Darfur region of Sudan has been manipulated by the imperialists to justify foreign intervention.

The attacks on China are not based on the ruling class's concern for children or product safety.

Although these organizations speak in the name of "human rights"—and never explicitly on behalf of the White House or the Pentagon—their criticisms of China are deeply political. China has emerged as a major player in African development projects, and likewise, in African politics.

China has no reason to fear independent economic development in other countries. For the imperialists, it is not enough to receive a large share of the raw materials and resources through trade. They need to be able to control how those resources are distributed. They do not simply seek an exchange of goods and services; they seek to dominate the development and destiny of all African countries. It is all done to maximize profit for the imperialists and their backers.

China is motivated primarily by a desire to have access to resources from Africa. It also seeks to develop bilateral relations with many African governments to counter the influence of U.S., British and French imperialism.

ONGOING CLASS STRUGGLE

In today's stage of modern monopoly capitalism, the imperialist nations—led by the United States—are on the offensive, seeking to reduce any obstacle or barrier that obstructs their ability to set up shop and exploit the labor, land and resources of the planet.

To the extent that the Chinese government has "opened up" the country for vast exploitation and profit making by transnational corporations, the imperialists view it as a "friend"—at least compared, for instance, to China in the Mao era.

To the extent that the Chinese government exists, however, as an entity independent of imperialism—not beholden to the dictates of Wall Street or the White House, for example—it is targeted for demonization. If the Chinese government pursues and defends China's national interests and refuses to become a neo-colonial puppet regime—imagine that!—the imperialist governments will seek to keep China on the defensive.

Hypocritical anti-China attacks by the U.S. capitalist press, Congress and the labor union leadership are meant to draw the working people of the United States into a campaign of scapegoating, hatred and national chauvinism. It is a dead-end that must be militantly opposed within the labor movement and also in the broader social movement. ☐

Tibet, imperialism and the right of self-determination

BY HEATHER BENNO

A**SKED** to describe their image of Tibet, most in the West would give the Hollywood version of reality: a nation of peace and spiritual harmony, where gentle monks live humbly side-by-side with a rustic peasant population at one with nature. In this image, it is hard to imagine the need for a government with a population so docile and free of conflict.

This image has been propagated by the imperialist media. It is contrasted with the counter-image of peaceful Tibetans brutally repressed by Chinese troops. In fact, public awareness of Tibet in general rises and falls with the periodic anti-China demonization campaigns conducted by the U.S. State Department and its agents.

This view fails to reflect the reality of Tibetan workers and peasants under the theocratic political rule of the Dalai Lama, the title of the traditional Tibetan head of state, who is supposedly the reincarnation of a spiritual leader from the 14th century. That rule ended abruptly in 1959, when the Dalai Lama's troops based on Tibetan landowners and elites were defeated by the Chinese Peoples' Liberation Army.

Tibet is an autonomous region of China, meaning that it is an integral part of China and is under the ultimate authority of the Beijing government, but enjoys wide self-governing powers. Tibetans are among the approximately 56 distinct nationalities in China. Within Tibet, other nationalities include Moinbas, Lhobas, Naxis, Huis, Dengs and Sherpas.

Few in the United States would know that the elected chair of Tibet's regional government is Qiangba Puncog, a former factory worker who joined the Communist Party of China in 1974 and spent his life in public service. Instead, U.S. propaganda has been such that

Tibet is almost synonymous with the Dalai Lama, the head of the "Tibetan Government in Exile."

This so-called government in exile, representing the former religious ruling class, is fully funded and supported by the United States. U.S. imperialist politicians and spokespeople routinely show their support for the Dalai Lama as a way of diplomatically needling the Chinese government. For example, on Oct. 17, 2007, the U.S. Congress awarded the Dalai Lama the Congressional Gold Medal of Honor—the U.S. government's "highest civilian honor."

When Iraq war supporters and supporters of militarizing the U.S.-Mexican border portray the Dalai Lama as "a unifying voice for global peace" and a holy man, the truth must be quite different. That can be seen by looking at the historical record of those who now try to speak in the name of Tibetan people.

THEOCRATIC RULE

Tibet became part of the Chinese empire in the 13th century, when it was conquered by Genghis Khan. Life in Tibet in the subsequent centuries was characterized by Buddhist clan fighting and feudal economic relations.

The Dalai Lama with his patron

The political rule of the Dalai Lamas began in 1578. The Dalai Lamas were like god-kings, using their religious authority alongside brutal repression to govern Tibet. In 1660, for example, the fifth Dalai Lama directed the Mongol army to "obliterate the male and female lines, and the offspring too 'like eggs smashed against rocks. ... In short, annihilate any traces of them, even their names.'"[1]

In his book "Buddha's Not Smiling: Uncovering Corruption at the Heart of Tibetan Buddhism Today," Erik D. Curren describes life under the Dalai Lamas: "History belies the Shangri-La image of Tibetan lamas and their followers living together in mutual tolerance and nonviolent goodwill. Old Tibet was much more like Europe during the religious wars of the Counterreformation."[2]

Tibet under the lamas was characterized by feudal economic and social relations. The source of power and wealth was land. Land, in turn, was divided among the monasteries, the nobility and the Lhasa government.

Tibet is 70 percent grassland and its economy has always been agricultural. Until 1959, most of the arable land was organized into manorial estates. These estates were owned by elite landowners or rich monasteries and were worked by serfs. Most rich monasteries amassed wealth through active participation in trade, commerce and money lending. Children were conscripted from poor families against their will to join monasteries at a young age and work for life.

Second in political power to the lamas was a feudal hereditary aristocracy. Most descended from an aristocracy dating back to before the Mongolian invasion. The commander-in-chief of the Tibetan army, a member of the Dalai Lama's cabinet, owned 4,000 square kilometers of land and 3,500 serfs.[3]

The vast majority of Tibetans were serfs or peasants. Others occupied lower ranks in the social hierarchy as slaves and beggars. Serfs faced a lifetime of servitude at the disposal of lords and the monasteries. They were bound to the land without pay and they had no access to education or medical care. Serfs raised livestock and field crops and transported their lords on demand. They could not even choose to marry without the consent of a lord or a lama.

Serfs were heavily taxed by both the aristocratic landowners and monasteries. Taxes supported the rule of the theocracy. Serfs were taxed upon marriage, childbirth and death. Taxes were also levied for, among other activities, planting trees, keeping animals, religious festivals, going to prison, being unemployed and travel. If the taxes were not paid, the debt was either handed down to family members or paid by a monastery at up to 50 percent interest. Those who could not pay faced slavery.[4]

IMPERIALIST INTERESTS

Entering the 20th century, Asia was a battleground for the world imperialist powers. Tibet was no exception. In addition to its forest and mineral wealth and proximity to oil, Tibet occupied a strategic geopolitical place in Asia. Tibet borders India and Nepal to the south. British and U.S imperialism looked to Tibet as a gateway to the heart of China.

In 1904, British troops from India invaded Tibet. Maj. Francis Younghusband led an expedition to seize Lhasa, carrying out several massacres along the way. After seizing the capital, Younghusband forced officials there to sign a treaty recognizing British mercantile interests in Tibet. In 1906, the British imposed similar terms on the disintegrating Chinese regime. China had by that time been forced to sign unequal treaties with all the imperialist powers.

In 1911, the Chinese empire collapsed in the face of a revolutionary military uprising. In 1912, Sun Yat-sen declared China a republic. In the power struggles that followed, central authority weakened as power was dispersed to various warlords across China. Tibet essentially functioned as an separate entity—still under the protection of Britain—although no government in the world recognized independence.

AFTER THE REVOLUTION

The victory of the 1949 Chinese Revolution marked a turning point for Tibet. In 1949, the Communist Party of China had drafted a constitution that included the provision that "all Mongolians, Tibetans, Miao, Yao, Koreans and others living in the territory of China shall enjoy the full rights to self-determination."

No area constituted a greater challenge for the communists than Tibet. The CPC had decades of practical experiences in dealing with the complicated problems of building unity with the many oppressed peoples and nationalities throughout China. During the historic Long March of 1935, Mao led the 7,000-plus-mile retreat from southern China. In each region, with the exception of Tibet, the communist-led Red Army was able to negotiate terms of friendship with the national minorities, who provided food and shelter for the retreating peasant army.

In Tibet, the local population was still so much under the domination of the religious ruling class that the communists made little progress. The Red Army was met with so much hostility that they could not buy food from the local populace and thus they had to forcibly procure what they needed to survive. Mao described these problems to the world-famous chronicler of the Chinese revolution, Edgar Snow.

"This is our only foreign debt, and some day we must pay the Mantzu (sic) and the Tibetans for the provisions we were obliged to take from them."[5]

It is likely that China would have proceeded very cautiously with the introduction of central government control, and especially socialist measures in Tibet, had it not been for international factors. Shortly after the United States invaded Korea in June 1950 under the mantle of the United Nations, the Tibetan ruling-class political parties appealed to the same United Nations to intervene in Tibet.

Ironically, the Soviet Union was boycotting the U.N. Security Council as a protest against the refusal to seat the People's Republic of China in the Security Council following the 1949 victory. Thus, the United Nations was turned into a complete puppet for U.S. foreign policy. At the same time that China was preparing to send more than a million soldiers to fight against advancing U.S. troops on its eastern border in late 1950, it made the decision to also move its army into Tibet on its western border.

In 1950, the first units of the People's Liberation Army entered Tibet. As the first presence of Chinese authority in nearly 40 years, the revolutionary army was initially greeted with distrust. Tibetan lords and monasteries in particular feared the new armies, because they feared that the Chinese communists would redistribute land and endow serfs and slaves with rights.

But the Chinese communists came armed with a Leninist position on national minorities—expressed in their recognition of the right to self-determination—and the class loyalties of peasants of all nationalities. When Tibetan aristocrats tried to militarily block the PLA from entering Tibet, most of the peasant troops defected and crossed to the side of the communist troops.

In May 1951, Tibetan and Chinese leaders signed the "Agreement of the Central People's Government and the Tibetan Local Government on Measures for Peaceful Liberation of Tibet." This agreement, known as the 17-Point Agreement, recognized that "the Tibetan people shall be united and drive out the imperialist aggressive forces from Tibet; that the people of Tibet shall return to the big family of the mother-land, the People's Republic of China." Guided by the principle of self-determination, the agreement recognized the rule of the Dalai Lama and the freedom of religion. It further recognized and promoted the Tibetan language and culture.

Over the next years, a class struggle emerged in Tibet based on the continued existence of the old feudal ruling class coexisting with the Chinese revolution's advancing of workers' and peasants' rights. The new revolutionary central government concentrated its efforts and resources on building schools, roads and highways in Tibet. The Chinese also distributed newspapers and introduced telephone and postal service. Communists built hospitals and health clinics in rural regions of Tibet where people had never seen health care. Interest rates were reduced, although the communists did not initially confiscate any estates.[6]

As land reform efforts gained momentum, however, the hostility of the Tibetan feudal lords mounted. Meanwhile, U.S. and British imperialists saw the opportunity to regain influence in the region and at the same time roll back communist influence.

Beginning in the early 1950s, the U.S. Central Intelligence Agency began to train counterrevolutionary military units in Tibet. Many of those recruited were members of the former elite. Gyalo Thondup, for example, the Dalai Lama's older brother, coordinated military action with the CIA from a U.S. base in India and Nepal.[7]

In 1956-57, CIA-trained rebel forces in Tibet attacked a PLA outpost in Lhasa.[8] The rebel militias disintegrated, however, failing to win public support. In March 1959, landlord-backed rebels marched into Lhasa, killing or wounding anyone suspected of cooperating with the revolutionary government. Despite this, PLA troops stayed in their barracks for 10 days.

Journalist Anna Louise Strong reports the explanation she was given by PLA officials:

"The 'kasha' was still the lawful government and the people of Lhasa had not yet taken sides. In such situations, our strategy is always never to start or develop the fighting but let the enemy start it and continue it until it is fully clear to all people who are the aggressors and the destroyers of law. Then, when we counter attack, we have the people with us, their support shortens the fighting and lessens the casualties in the end. The rebels lost the people of Lhasa in those ten days."[9]

Following the failure of this reactionary armed uprising in 1959, the Dalai Lama fled to India to establish a new "government in exile." The Chinese government recognized the authority of the second most influential lama, the Panchen Lama, in the Dalai Lama's absence. Former serfs voted for the first time ever in 1961. In 1965, China recognized the Tibetan Autonomous Region.

From the early 1960s until 1973, "Khamba" contras carried out attacks on Tibet from bases in the Walanchung-gola and Mustang regions of Nepal. The "Tibetan Government in Exile" received approximately $1.7 million per year from the CIA. Contras were airlifted into Tibet for attacks against the government.[10]

In the subsequent decade, the religious theocracy was dismantled, bringing about a very different social structure in Tibet. Slavery was abolished, many of the taxes were eliminated and serfs were given paid employment on new civic projects, such as establishing running water and building infrastructure.

THE FRUITS OF LIBERATION

Today, monasteries are open in Tibet and monks are free to practice their religion. In the new social structure, religion is no longer used as an instrument of repression.

Economic development, a goal for all of China, has been even more vital in Tibet as one of the most underdeveloped regions of an underdeveloped country. Gross domestic production grew by a factor of 30 between 1951 and 2000. In 1950, there was a single 125-kilowatt power station in the entire region; in 2000, there were 401 power plants producing 356,200 kilowatts.

In pre-revolution Tibet, there were no schools at all. Education was the sole province of the monasteries. By 2000, 86 percent of school-age children were enrolled in schools.

Even relative to the rest of China, conditions in Tibet are becoming comparable. In 2000, the number of hospital beds and doctors per thousand population is higher than for China overall.[11]

None of these gains would have been possible under the old imperialist-backed ruling class.

In fact, it is precisely regions like Tibet—among China's least developed regions—that stand to lose the most in the event of a counterrevolution in China. Tibetans would find themselves in the position of the citizens of the Caucasus or other poorer republics of the former Soviet Union, who have seen unemployment and poverty skyrocket since the restoration of capitalist rule in 1991.

Tibetan workers and peasants—like workers and peasants from the other national minorities in China—undoubtedly weigh the benefits of unity with China against the exiles' misleading promises of the green pastures of independence.

For that reason, socialists and progressive people have nothing in common with the "Tibetan government in exile" or the Dalai Lama. □

Endnotes

1. Michael Parenti, "Friendly Feudalism: The Tibet Myth," www. michaelparenti.org/Tibet.html.
2. Erik Curren, *Buddha's Not Smiling* (Alaya Press, 2005), 41.
3. Parenti, op. cit.
4. Ibid.
5. Edgar Snow, *Red Star Over China* (Grove Press, 1968), 203-204.
6. Parenti, op. cit.
7. Ibid.
8. Ibid.
9. Anna Louis Strong, *Tibetan Interviews* (New World Press: Peking, 1959), 30.
10. Parenti, op. cit.
11. Information Office of the State Council of the People's Republic of China "Tibet's March to Modernization," *China Daily*, March 2001.

Still awaiting reunification

Fortress Taiwan: Imperialism's front line against China

BY SARAH SLOAN

"**W**E are all convinced that our work will go down in the history of mankind, demonstrating that the Chinese people, comprising one quarter of humanity, have now stood up. ... Ours will no longer be a nation subject to insult and humiliation. We have stood up. Our revolution has won the sympathy and acclaim of the people of all countries. We have friends all over the world."

Those were some of the words in the opening address of Chinese Communist Party chairman Mao Zedong at the First Plenary Session of the Chinese People's Political Consultative Conference on Sept. 21, 1949.

Mao repeated the declaration that "the Chinese people have stood up" when he proclaimed the establishment of the People's Republic of China 10 days later. Those words have gone down in history because they so deeply reflected the sentiment of the Chinese people, as well as the working class and the oppressed of the world, about the victory of the Chinese Revolution.

This same sentiment was demonstrated again in 1971 when the delegates of the United Nations rose to their feet in a standing ovation following the two-thirds vote to approve U.N. General Assembly Resolution 2758 recognizing the People's Republic of China as the sole legitimate representative of the Chinese people in this international body. For the previous 22 years, the Nationalist Party (Kuomintang or KMT) government led by Chiang Kai-shek occupied the U.N. seat even after the defeat of the KMT and the victory of the revolution in 1949.

THE QUESTION OF REUNIFICATION

Today, the future of the 14,000-square-mile island known as Taiwan, situated 75 miles off the southeastern coast of mainland China, remains a matter of struggle. Taiwan is formally known as the "Republic of China."

In Taiwan, the KMT no longer occupies the highest political offices. It officially advocates reunification with mainland China—on the basis of the overthrow of the Chinese government and a KMT takeover of the mainland. Taiwan's Democratic Progressive Party favors more bourgeois democratic rights compared to the KMT's semi-fascist orientation. The DPP advocates for independence for Taiwan, looking toward a greater alliance with Japanese imperialism.

The KMT and DPP are the two main bourgeois parties campaigning in Taiwan's 2008 presidential elections. Neither promotes a political program that reflects the interests and rights of the Chinese working class and peasantry. Both parties function as tools for U.S. imperialism, with the DPP representing the native Taiwanese bourgeoisie that has developed since 1949 and the KMT representing the traditional bourgeoisie ousted from the mainland and transplanted onto the island.[1]

Due to the particular history of Taiwan since 1949, when it became a fortress for U.S.-backed counterrevolution, Chinese workers in Taiwan have challenges in forging an anti-imperialist movement for reunification with their mainland sisters and brothers.

THE HISTORY OF TAIWAN AND IMPERIALISM

Immigration of Chinese people from the mainland to the island now known as Taiwan began as early as the 13th century, growing more rapidly beginning in the 16th century. Today, about 84 percent of the island's population descends from these early immigrants. Another 14 percent of the population descends from those who left the mainland after the victory of the revolution in 1949. The remaining 2 percent of the population are indigenous, descendants of those native to the island prior to Chinese immigration. Those small numbers are the result in large part of a genocidal campaign carried out by Japanese colonizers in the first half of the 20th century.[2]

Taiwan was considered a part of China beginning in the 16th century.[3] It exists today as a separate entity only because of imperialism.

Though Japan sought colonial domination of the island as early as the late 16th century, it remained an extension of the Chinese mainland until Japan's victory in 1895 during what became known as the First Sino-Japanese War. Taiwan was a colony of Japan from 1895 until Japan's defeat in World War II. The island was returned to China, a validation of the worldwide and historical recognition of the relationship between the mainland and the island.

The KMT took over governing Taiwan from the Japanese in 1945. At that time, the KMT was involved in a brutal civil war against the communist Red Army on the mainland.

KMT terror took place in Taiwan as well, most notably in the "228 Massacre." On Feb. 28, 1947, the KMT government killed as many as 30,000 people—including many communists and other progressives—to put down a rebellion. Chiang Kai-shek is widely believed to have directly ordered this suppression.[4]

Nationalist forces used Taiwan as a base to launch this bombing attack on Shanghai in 1951.

Following the Oct. 1, 1949 victory of the Chinese Revolution, an estimated 1.3 million opponents of the revolution moved from the mainland to the island. This vast exodus was a virtual takeover of the island from its original population. It included KMT members, officials and soldiers, members of the Chinese bourgeois and landlord class and petty-bourgeois businesspeople and intellectuals.

To secure its grip on the island, the KMT imposed military rule. In fact, martial law was in place until 1987. During this period known as the "white terror," almost 150,000 people were imprisoned or executed for alleged opposition to the KMT.[5] These fascistic conditions drove communists and all progressive people and organizations on the island underground. It was impossible to form organizations or movements advocating reunification with the mainland on a progressive basis, although such sentiment existed.

THE ROLE OF U.S. IMPERIALISM

From the 1949 KMT takeover until today, U.S. imperialism has viewed the island as an important part of its efforts to overthrow the Chinese Revolution. This has remained the case despite the 1971 seating of the People's Republic of China in the United Nations. It is the case despite the 1972 Shanghai Communiqué, in which the U.S. government acknowledged the People's Republic's "one-China principle" of not recognizing the KMT as the government of a separate political entity and agreed to begin withdrawing troops from the island. It is the case despite the 1979 Joint Communiqué in which the United States and China established formal diplomatic relations.

Because of these pacts, the U.S. government has no formal diplomatic recognition of Taiwan and no direct military presence. Yet in many ways, the U.S. policy toward China was best summarized by Gen. Douglas MacArthur in 1950: in the hands of an opponent, Taiwan would be an "unsinkable aircraft carrier and submarine tender."[6]

In 1979, four months after the U.S. government formally recognized the People's Republic, it passed the Taiwan Relations Act. This act formalized quasi-diplomatic relations between the United States and Taiwan. It has been used to justify massive U.S. arms sales to Taiwan since its passage. China considers the act to be interference in their internal affairs and a hindrance to national reunification.

The act also established the American Institute in Taiwan, a nominally private enterprise that is in fact the official U.S. State Department presence in Taiwan. In this way, the U.S. Congress and executive branch continue close diplomatic, military and economic ties with Taiwan.

The 1991 National Security Strategy proposed "strong, unofficial, substantive relations" between the United States and Taiwan. In 2000, Congress passed the Taiwan Security Enhancement Act, reinforcing the relationship established two decades earlier. The 2003 Foreign Relations Authorization Act required that Taiwan be treated as a "major non-NATO ally" for the purpose of sales under U.S. arms export control laws, affording Taiwan preference over China regarding sales of many items, including high-powered computers and "dual-use" goods—items that can have both a civilian and military use.

U.S. weapons sales to Taiwan have always been substantial and have increased in the last 15 years. In the 1980s and 1990s, sales totaled almost $40 billion. In 1992, the United States sold Taiwan 150 F-16 fighters totaling $6 billion. This huge arms sale exceeded the limits of a 1982 communiqué between the United States and China, which precluded a substantial increase in sales.[7]

Between 1994 and 1999 alone, Taiwan imported $13.3 billion worth of arms, 95 percent of them from the United States. This made Taiwan the world's biggest arms importer. In 1998, Taiwan was the second highest recipient of U.S. military exports, only receiving less than Saudi Arabia. These exports totaled over $1.6 billion,[8] more than U.S. military exports to Israel, South Korea and Egypt, all more well-known recipients of U.S. weaponry.

Geography shows the reason for such a large U.S. military presence in Taiwan. With a direct U.S. military presence in South Korea and Japan to the north of Taiwan, and in the Philippines to the south, the island would be a critical launching point for U.S. military operations. As Gen. MacArthur noted, the loss of Taiwan would be a major vulnerability.

Stephen M. Young, the director of the American Institution in Taiwan and therefore the de facto U.S. ambassador to Taiwan, described the current U.S. view at a Nov. 9, 2007 press conference:

"On the security front, we have since 1979, under the Taiwan Relations Act, developed effective mechanisms to support Taiwan's efforts to defend itself against any external threat," Young stated. "This has included, specifically, critical infrastructure protection, greater jointness or cooperation between the military services, the maintenance of adequate stockpiles of armaments and supplies and the development of a noncommissioned officer corps. At the same time, we continue to see the mainland's rapid buildup across the Strait as a force for instability and a threat to the status quo, and we raise this in our discussions regularly with Beijing."[9]

Referring to the People's Republic of China as a "force for instability and a threat to the status quo" is just double-speak. The People's Republic is depicted as an aggressor for insisting that it has the right to make preparations to defend itself against the U.S.-Taiwan-Japan military alliance and threats. This propaganda is then used to justify the obscene quantities of military weapons that Taiwan buys from the United States.

Groups, like the Anti-Arms Trade Alliance,[10] in Taiwan are trying to build mass opposition to the huge U.S. weapons sales that have turned the island into a fortress.

WHICH WAY FORWARD?

The political status of Taiwan is an internal matter for the Chinese government in Beijing and the Chinese people. Communists support the right of nations to self-determination, including the right to secede to independence, as an integral step toward building multinational unity against capitalism and imperialism. But when the imperialists become the champions of self-determination and independence, it is inevitably part of some larger divide-and-conquer scheme.

Taiwan's fate cannot be separated from the issue of the colonialism imposed on the Chinese people. The return of Taiwan to China is understood by the Chinese government as an unresolved issue from the colonial era. In that sense, it is seen as fundamental to China's long struggle for national liberation.

Integrating such a strong capitalist economy will of course pose a challenge for the Communist Party of China leadership. There is also the political challenge of contending with the most reactionary of Chinese political forces, and raising the political consciousness and the level of mobilization of Chinese people living on the island.

The Chinese government approaches these problems, however, with the experience of the return of the former British colony of Hong Kong to Chinese sovereignty in 1997. That transfer took place with little unrest or disruption of lives.

Reunification with Taiwan carries the political threat of strengthening the hand of pro-capitalist restorationist elements within the CPC. Because of the social weight of the Taiwanese bourgeoisie—which is much more linked to U.S. imperialism than to the Chinese capitalists—efforts to create compromise or "peaceful coexistence" can only pull the political center of gravity to the right.

Having said that, in its current state configuration, Taiwan serves as a base for U.S. imperialism for its past and future efforts supporting those who seek to overthrow the Chinese government. It is a means for U.S. and Japanese imperialism to strengthen their domination over East Asia. This is a far greater danger than the political challenges posed by reunification. □

The writer traveled to Taiwan (China) in 2003 to attend events hosted by the Labor Rights Association and Labor Party, working-class organizations advocating reunification and opposition to U.S. and Japanese imperialism.

Endnotes

1. Labor Rights Association, "The Deepening General Social Crisis in Neocolonial Taiwan," Taiwan Area Report to the 10th Asia Wide Campaign (AWC) Campaign Coordinating Body (CCB), November 2001.

2. See, for example, "Taiwanese Hardliner Visits Japan's War Shrine," Agence France Presse, April 5, 2005; "TSU Chairman's Visit to Yasukuni Shrine Protested," *China Post*, April 5, 2005.

3. Taiwan Affairs Office & Information Office, State Council, The People's Republic of China "The Taiwan Question and Reunification of China," Beijing: August 1993.

4. For an account of the 228 massacre, see, Tillman Durdin "Formosa killings are put at 10,000," *New York Times*, March 29, 1947; Peggy Durdin; "Terror in Taiwan," *The Nation*, May 24, 1947.

5. Ko Shu-Ling,"The 228 Incident: Sixty years on—Sixty years on, answers remain elusive," *Taipei Times*, February 28, 2007.

"A private group dedicated to investigating the early years of the White Terror era, from 1949 to 1954, placed the number of deaths at 4,000. The group estimated 150,000 people were jailed and 120,000 went missing."

6. Statement by Douglas MacArthur to the Fifty-First National Encampment of the Veterans of Foreign Wars, August 20, 1950.

7. Labor Rights Association "The Deepening General Social Crisis in Neocolonial Taiwan."

8. David Lockhead and James Morrell, "Arms Trade: U.S. Outsells All Others Combined" *Center for International Policy,* November 2000.

9. Stephen M. Young, director, American Institute in Taiwan Official "Transcript of press conference at the AIT American Cultural Center," Taipei, November 9, 2007.

10. Ko Shu-Ling, "Anti-arms Alliance Plans Protest at Legislative Yuan," *Taipei Times,* September 25, 2005.

Tiananmen Square 1989

Facing the threat of counterrevolution

BY YENICA CORTES

FOR partisans of socialism—and especially for those who want to defend the efforts of those trying to build socialism in the countries where revolutions have displaced the political rule of the capitalist class—recognizing counterrevolutionary efforts is essential. Since 1848, when socialism first appeared on the world stage, history has shown that the capitalist class never permits revolutionaries a moment's rest in trying to extinguish the working class's efforts to advance its rights.

It would be easy to spot counterrevolutionary efforts if they always appeared as evil villains, CIA agents and rich corporate executives. The class struggle is not so simple, however.

The faces of counterrevolution in Chile in 1973 were "normal" middle-class housewives. The face of counterrevolution in Poland in the 1980s was a "union" leader named Lech Walesa. In 1991, the face of counterrevolution in the Soviet Union was a Communist Party functionary named Boris Yeltsin.

It has been nearly 20 years since the Chinese government suppressed a mass student demonstration in Tiananmen Square, Beijing's main plaza, in 1989. The image of that event is still used to this day as evidence of the sinister character of the Chinese government.

In spite of the massive propaganda campaign against the Chinese government in the aftermath of the Tiananmen demonstrations, the facts of the events are generally recognized today to be in accord with the Chinese government's description. More importantly, the political character of that demonstration was clearly aimed at the overthrow of the Communist Party of China—and its replacement not by a more progressive government of the working class and peasants—but by a

U.S.-oriented clique of relatively privileged students and bureaucrats who hoped to restore capitalism in China.

INTERNATIONAL CONTEXT

The world context for the Tiananmen Square demonstrations was the shift taking place within the Communist Party of the Soviet Union. In 1985, Mikhail Gorbachev became the general secretary of the CPSU. Responding to the tremendous pressure to match U.S. imperialism in military spending, Gorbachev announced a program of reforms beginning in 1986. The political reforms became known as "glasnost" (openness), and were touted as an effort to break out of the CPSU "orthodoxy." The economic reforms were known as "perestroika" (restructuring), and amounted to efforts to introduce market mechanisms and de-emphasize economic planning.

Gorbachev unfolded his program between 1986 and 1989 to the cheers of world imperialism. In 1984, shortly before Gorbachev took office and while he was a Politburo member, conservative and viciously anti-labor British prime minister Margaret Thatcher tipped her hand by declaring: "I like him." He was named Time magazine's "Man of the Year" in 1987 and again in 1989.

Politically, Gorbachev's program energized pro-capitalist and pro-imperialist elements inside and outside of the ruling communist parties in Eastern Europe and within the Soviet Union. The U.S. government and media, as well as pseudo-private groups like George Soros' Open Society Institute, took advantage of Gorbachev's reforms to engineer mass support for counterrevolution.

IMPACT IN CHINA

China had severed political ties with the Soviet Union long ago. Despite the fact that communist parties governed both countries, the political struggles between them beginning in the late 1950s had effectively broken any bond between them.

Nevertheless, Gorbachev's economic reforms shared many common features with the reforms that began nearly 10 years earlier in China. Both relied on elements of the capitalist market, both relied on a de-emphasis of economic planning and a reliance on enterprise profit as the criteria for investment.

There was an important difference, however, between the Soviet and Chinese experience.

The Gorbachev leadership lost control of the process and was overthrown by pro-capitalist elements inside of the Soviet leadership. Boris Yeltsin was the spokesperson and organizer of this trend inside the Politburo of the Communist Party of the Soviet Union. As a leading member of the Politburo, he was brought in by Gorbachev as an advocate of perestroika. But Yeltsin's goal was to eliminate socialism altogether.

The Chinese version of perestroika was implemented within tight bounds administered by the Chinese Communist Party. The Soviet policy of glasnost had the effect of emboldening those who saw the reforms as a way to overthrow the existing government and replace it with a regime of unfettered capitalism.

> *The political character of the Tiananmen demonstration was clearly aimed at the overthrow of the Communist Party of China.*

The same phenomena repeated itself in China—but with a far different outcome.

China's version of Boris Yeltsin was Secretary General Hu Yaobang, who was widely seen as a proponent of pushing the reforms ahead at a faster pace until his resignation in 1987.

The death of Hu Yaobang on April 15, 1989, was one of the factors that triggered the protests in Tiananmen Square that ultimately led to the government crackdown on June 4, 1989.

Despite the fact that the Chinese reforms were more cautiously implemented than those in the Soviet Union, they created the social basis for the Tiananmen Square demonstrations. They had allowed many elements of the CPC, who had been purged during China's Cultural Revolution as rightists, to return to privileged positions. Many of China's youth had been sent abroad to study, exposing them to intense bourgeois propaganda in the privileged setting of elite U.S. and European universities.

THE TIANANMEN EVENTS

Two events triggered the Tiananmen Square protests. On April 15, 1989, Hu Yaobang died. Pro-capitalist reform elements within the CPC used the mourning of Hu's death as a public demonstration that was widely seen as an attempt to expand the reforms. Students at Beijing's elite universities took up the call and announced protests in Tiananmen Square beginning on April 18.

Tens of thousands of students came out in the days leading up to Hu's funeral on April 22. At that point, the main demands centered around "freedom" and "democracy."

The second factor that fueled the demonstrations was Mikhail Gorbachev's visit to Beijing on May 15. It was the first visit by a Soviet leader to China since 1959. Those who favored the capitalist-oriented reforms saw the visit as a further chance to press their demands both within the CPC and in front of the world media.

Two days before the Gorbachev visit, students launched a hunger strike, hardening their position relative to the government.

During this time, the Tiananmen demonstration was becoming a focal point for general discontent. Workers joined the protests in limited numbers, raising demands against corruption, inflation and unemployment generated by the capitalist-oriented reforms. These demands, however, were demagogically tolerated by the counter-revolutionary thrust of the student leaders and their supporters within the CPC.

MARTIAL LAW

After weeks of unsuccessfully trying to negotiate with the protest leaders, including visits by senior leaders to the square itself, the CPC leadership declared martial law on May 20. By this time, the number of students in the square was diminishing, with many of those who had traveled to Beijing from other parts of the country returning to their homes.

The student leaders who remained in the square were pushing for a harder line with the government. On May 28, Chai Ling, who many of the students acknowledged as the "commander-in-chief" of the Tiananmen demonstrations, stated that the student leadership's goal was to provoke the Communist Party into attacking the demonstrators.

"I feel so sad," Chai sobbed to U.S. reporter Philip Cunningham. "How can I tell [the students in the Square] that what we are actually hoping for is bloodshed, the moment when the government is ready to butcher the people brazenly? Only when the Square is awash in blood will the people of China open their eyes. Only then will they be really united."

The bloodshed Chai and her fellow leaders hoped for did in fact take place. But it did not have the intended impact.

On June 2, unarmed People's Liberation Army troops were called in to regain control of the square. Students left the square to confront the troops in the streets leading to the square. Some of the unarmed troops were taken hostage.

On June 3, the soldiers were issued arms—"though under orders to avoid violence" as reported in a June 5 article in the Wall Street Journal. On June 4, however, demonstrators resorted to violent attacks on soldiers as protesters grabbed hold of army equipment and seized weapons.

The Chinese government denounced the attacks as counterrevolutionary and ordered the People's Liberation Army to retake the square. Although there were clashes with troops in the streets leading up to the square, most students left the square peacefully before the PLA troops arrived to establish order. The Chinese government reported that some 300 people, both students and PLA soldiers, had been killed in the clashes outside the square.

The pro-imperialist media responded by unleashing a wild propaganda campaign condemning the Chinese government. Every big-business media outlet in the world blared reports of the PLA killing "tens of thousands" of demonstrators. The media created a story of a "massacre" of innocent, peaceful student protesters run down by tanks in the square.

SETTING THE RECORD STRAIGHT

It took several years to set the record straight, although reports of the true extent of the incident began to come out within weeks.

Television footage of the days' events shows rioters taunting soldiers, taking their rifles, firebombing tanks and buses with soldiers still inside, pulling soldiers out from trucks and severely beating and killing them.

A June 12, 1989, article in the Wall Street Journal reported, "Aerial pictures of the conflagration and columns of smoke have powerfully bolstered the [Chinese] government's arguments that the troops were victims, not executioners."

On June 13, 1989, New York Times reporter Nicholas Kristof reported, "there is no firm indication that troops fired on students" occupying the Square itself, but rather the fighting had taken place in the streets outside the square.

In a Jan. 16, 1990, article by Kristof, students and pop singer Hou Dejian, who were present on June 4, admitted seeing "no one killed in Tiananmen Square." According to Dejian, the 3,000 students remaining in the square were negotiating with the troops and decided to leave in the early morning hours. In the same article, it was declared that 300 people were killed in fights in the streets leading up to the square, many of whom were soldiers of the People's Liberation Army.

Of course, these accounts came after the Western media had repeatedly characterized the events in Tiananmen Square as a "massacre of students."

THE POLITICAL CHARACTER
OF THE TIANANMEN DEMONSTRATIONS

There were a large number of students involved in the demonstrations, but it is important to note that China's university students at the time made up only 0.2 percent of the country's population of 1.1 billion. And while there were many political trends within the student movement, there was a dominant leadership group. The goals of this group had nothing to do with democracy for China's vast majority of poor and working people.

Some claim that the student protesters had vague demands. But one force that understood the students' orientation very clearly was U.S. imperialism. Their signs were in English. Their symbol, the so-called "Goddess of Democracy," bore a striking resemblance to the Statue of Liberty. Many expressed their hope of founding a new student organization on July 4—Independence Day in the United States.

None of the students spoke in the name of internationalism, socialism or communism.

Wang Dan, one of the central leaders of the student movement, was quoted in the June 3 New York Times: "The movement is not ready for worker participation because the principles of democracy must first be absorbed by students and intellectuals before they can be spread to others." In a June 2, 1993, interview with the Washington Post, Dan goes further to say that "the pursuit of wealth [was] part of the impetus for democracy."

Clearly, he was not talking about workers' socialist democracy, where the needs of the people are met first and foremost. The quote—like those of other student leaders—gives a hint as to what they meant by "freedom": the freedom for China to open its market to capitalism, and consequently the freedom of the capitalist world market to exploit Chinese workers.

AFTERMATH

Much has changed since 1989. Gorbachev's policies led to the destruction of the socialist camp in the Soviet Union and Eastern Europe. Millions of workers in those countries now live like their counterparts around the world—facing unemployment, poverty and insecurity.

There was some hope that the Tiananmen Square protests would be a sign to those in the Communist Party of China that the reforms needed to be reversed. That has not happened. Instead, the reforms have accelerated to the point that a sizeable capitalist class now exists in China—far stronger than it was in 1989.

That raises the prospect that this new capitalist class will again raise its head in a bid for political power.

Whether the Communist Party of China still has enough credibility in the eyes of the Chinese workers and peasants to resist such an attempt will be seen in the course of the struggle. One thing is clear: The impact of a full-scale counterrevolution in China would make the misery that is sweeping the former socialist countries of Eastern Europe pale by comparison.

Imperialism will stop at nothing to put an end to the Chinese Revolution. For them, capitalist market "reforms" are not enough. They want unrestricted access to Chinese resources, markets and labor. Along with the growing bourgeois class in China, imperialist forces are intent on undermining whatever remains of the Chinese workers' state.

It is the duty of socialists and progressive people around the world not to be fooled by imperialist propaganda and to defend the achievements of the Chinese Revolution—regardless of disagreements with the CPC leadership. It would be the greatest crime to stand aside as over 1 billion Chinese workers and peasants were once again thrown to the mercy of unfettered imperialist exploitation—the inevitable outcome, under the current political circumstances, of the overthrow of the Chinese government. □

ISSUES FACING CHINA
AND SOCIALISM

Lenin and the New Economic Policy

Can market methods be used to build socialism?

BY CRYSTAL KIM

THE Communist Party of China's economic policies since 1978 have been carried out under the banner of building a "socialist market economy," also called "market socialism" or "socialism with Chinese characteristics." These formulations imply that certain features of the capitalist market—competition between enterprises instead of economic planning, the use of material incentives like bonuses to spur worker productivity and a reliance on foreign capital investment—can be used to develop what the Chinese government claims will be a socialist economy. Such a policy, the Chinese party claims, lays the basis for later socialist development through socialization and planning in the distant or not-so-distant future.

In fact, every country that has experienced a socialist revolution has resorted to a limited use of the capitalist market at times in their development. These measures were sometimes considered an economic retreat under dire circumstances, like the "Special Period in Time of Peace" in Cuba that began in 1991 in the wake of economic crisis following the overthrow of the Soviet Union.

V.I. Lenin and the Bolshevik Party faced the question of using capitalist economic measures soon after the victory of the 1917 Russian Revolution. In 1921, the Russian Communist Party introduced capitalist measures in an initiative called the New Economic Policy.

BACKGROUND TO THE NEP

In a 1921 report to the Second All-Russia Congress of Political Education Departments, Lenin summarized the Bolsheviks' perspective:

> At the beginning of 1918, we expected a period in
> which peaceful construction would be possible. When the

Brest peace [ending Russia's involvement in World War I] was signed it seemed that danger had subsided for a time and that it would be possible to start peaceful construction. But we were mistaken, because in 1918 a real military danger overtook us in the shape of the Czechoslovak mutiny and the outbreak of the civil war, which dragged on until 1920.[1]

The impact of the danger to which Lenin referred—which included three years of civil war and an imperialist invasion—is seen starkly when pre- and post-war production levels are compared. Production of steel had fallen from 4.2 million tons to 183,000 tons. The total harvest of grain had decreased from 801 million hundredweight to 503 million by 1922. Foreign trade had fallen from 2.9 billion rubles to 30 million rubles—a 100-fold drop.[2]

During the civil war, the new revolutionary government adopted what it referred to as "war communism," in which the old capitalist market was completely abolished. Goods in the countryside that were needed for industrial production were requisitioned by the government—if necessary, by the Red Army directly. Food and other necessities were distributed to the urban and rural population on the basis of need.

The food appropriation system in rural districts ultimately proved ineffective, especially after the most severe dangers of civil war had subsided. This, in turn, became a drag on reviving industrial production. Economic scarcity was so severe that the urban proletariat was abandoning the cities and returning to the countryside just to acquire food. Famine was rampant.

In looking for a way forward under these bleak circumstances, Lenin pointed to two possible outcomes. One was that the capitalists would take advantage of the situation and use it to overturn the 1917 revolution. The other outcome, Lenin argued, would be for the workers' state to reintroduce capitalism under its own terms to stimulate the economy and increase production. Lenin's 1921 report continued:

> The whole question is who will take the lead. We must face the issue squarely—who will come out on top? Either the capitalists succeed in organizing first—in which case they will drive out the Communists and that

will be the end of it. Or the proletarian state power, with the support of the peasantry, will prove capable of keeping a proper rein on those gentlemen, the capitalists, so as to direct capitalism along state channels and to create a capitalism that will be subordinate to the state and serve the state.[3]

According to this tactical orientation, capitalism was on the verge of reappearing in the Soviet Union—with or without the involvement of the proletarian state. Given those circumstances, the best option was for the state to harness the re-entrance of capitalism by setting the terms of its existence. They were bending so as not to break, as the classic saying goes. Thus, the NEP was inaugurated in 1921.

Lenin did not prettify the NEP as a Russian innovation on how best to build socialism. He called things by their right names and explained the danger of allowing the return of capitalist property relations. "The fight against capitalist society has become a hundred times more fierce and perilous, because we are not always able to tell enemies from friends," Lenin stated in a speech at the party's 11th Congress in 1922.[4]

AIMS OF THE NEP

The goals of the NEP were threefold. First, the NEP aimed to stimulate production in the countryside by restoring the capitalist market internally, substituting a tax for the surplus appropriation system. This was designed to give the peasantry—around 95 percent of the population—an incentive to increase production.

The NEP also denationalized many small enterprises. But because the workers' state had chosen to "take the lead" in restoring the capitalist market, it was possible at the same time to preserve state ownership of the basic means of production and complete control and sovereignty over foreign trade, thereby protecting the U.S.S.R. from imperialism.[5]

Second, the NEP aimed to rebuild the decimated industrial proletariat through the reintroduction of capitalist relations within the bounds of the workers' state. The proletariat class had nearly disappeared by the time the NEP was inaugurated as a result of the civil and imperialist war, and movement back to the countryside during the time of war communism. The creation of a new industrial proletariat would strengthen the base of the Soviet Union against the capitalist class—very important since the capitalists would ultimately try to use the NEP to smash the revolution.

Third, Lenin understood the NEP as a requisite for maintaining the alliance between the workers and peasants that had been forged in the heat of the 1917 revolution. The peasants, most of whom were small farmers, received virtually nothing from the Soviet state or state-owned industry during the civil war of 1917-20 because there was nothing to give. Everything went to the Red Army soldiers fighting at the front. Lenin's argument for the NEP was that the restoration of a limited capitalist market would help the peasants acquire what the state could not provide.

Another aspect of the NEP, in addition to market relations in the countryside and material incentives in the industries, was the effort to invite foreign capital to form joint ventures in Russia under favorable terms. This program had first been put in place shortly after the 1917 revolution, but with few exceptions the imperialists spurned the opportunity to invest between 1918 and 1920. Confident that the Soviet regime would collapse, they put their money on an all-sided invasion by 14 imperialist and allied armies.

Under the NEP, the proposal for foreign concessions was revived. Foreign capitalists were offered the opportunity to invest and reap huge profit from gold mining and oil extraction, timber, specialized industry and railway construction. Even western banks were offered the chance to extend loans to state-owned and private industry.

Lenin insisted, however, on the retention of the state's monopoly of foreign trade,[6] thus ensuring that the workers' state would keep foreign economic interests under close supervision. It is noteworthy that the general attitude of the western capitalist governments and corporations was to shun, boycott and impose economic sanctions rather than seek profits from investments in the U.S.S.R.

'A VERY SEVERE DEFEAT AND RETREAT'

The NEP achieved the goals set out for it within the course of just five years. Before the NEP, the output of large-scale industry had fallen to 14 percent of what it had been before the war.[7] By 1926, production had reached the pre-war level.[8]

Despite this success, the NEP was never meant to be more than a tactical retreat. In his repeated discussions on the policy, neither Lenin nor any of the other Bolshevik leaders ever claimed that the NEP was an advance in communist strategy or a kind of "socialism with Russian characteristics"—much less a permanent state of affairs.

In fact, Lenin characterized the NEP not as an advancement of socialism but as a necessary economic retreat to overcome famine and poverty. He wrote, "We had to take a step which from the point of view of our line, of our policy, cannot be called anything else than a very severe defeat and retreat." Lenin went further by calling capitalism and commodity exchange "the enemy in our midst."[10]

The NEP was a retreat, not only in principle but also in the reality of the class struggle. As a result of the NEP, unemployment re-emerged. Cleavages between rich, middle and poor peasants widened. Meanwhile, well-to-do peasants, called kulaks, and capitalists were pushing for more capitalist allowances.

Little by little, the economic gains of the NEP became overshadowed by the growing class antagonisms between rich peasants and "NEPmen"—merchants who took advantage of the new market to sell agricultural goods in the cities for inflated prices—on the one hand, and the poor peasants and working class on the other. In January 1928, the kulaks began to refuse to sell any food to the cities and demanded higher profits. The crisis that followed was a blow to those within the Soviet leadership who, after Lenin's death in 1924, became overly reliant on the NEP's capitalist methods.

The NEP was abolished in 1929. Socialist methods in the form of economic planning and collectivization resumed. But this did not take place without a severe struggle. Eight years of a "get rich" policy in the countryside meant that the struggle for collectivization—and in particular the struggle by poor peasants against newly rich landlords and kulaks—bordered on a new civil war. The kulaks and capitalist class were defeated, along with those who had hoped that the NEP would develop into the permanent reinstatement of capitalism.

NEP VERSUS 'MARKET SOCIALISM'

Lenin's candid assessment that the NEP was a step backward away from socialism has nothing in common with the Communist Party of China's glorification of "market socialism." What is happening in China is fundamentally different. The CPC does not speak in terms of a temporary retreat, but rather of a long-term policy of turning over already-nationalized and collectivized property to capitalist ownership. Public ownership still exists in large parts of the industrial sector. But many state-owned enterprises have been fully or partly privatized and operate on the basis of making profit.

Lenin's approach to the NEP had nothing to do with vulgar pragmatism—the notion that "whatever works is good." On the contrary, it was based on a careful assessment of the economic needs of the country measured against the balance of opposing class forces. It was based on an honest explanation of the policy, calling a retreat by its name.

The CPC certainly does not refer to its "market socialism" policies as a retreat. It will be seen in upcoming struggles whether those in the party leadership who are still committed to the socialist project have correctly assessed the strength of the new capitalist class. □

Endnotes

1. V.I. Lenin, "The New Economic Policy and the Tasks of the Political Education Departments," in *Collected Works*, vol. 33 (Moscow: Progress Publishers, 1973), 62.
2. Leon Trotsky, *The Revolution Betrayed* (New York: Pathfinder Press, 1937), 22.
3. Lenin, *Collected Works*, vol. 33, 66.
4. V.I. Lenin, "Political report of the Central Committee of the R.C.P. (B.), Eleventh Congress of the R.C.P. (B.), March 27, 1922," in *Collected Works*, vol. 33, 287.
5. Sam Marcy, *Perestroika* (New York: WW Publishers, 1990), 80.
6. "The Congress categorically affirms that the monopoly of foreign trade is immutable and that no one is permitted to bypass it or waver in implementing it. The new Central Committee is instructed to take systematic measures to strengthen and promote the monopoly of foreign trade." Resolution of the R.C.P. (B.) Twelfth Congress, April 17-25, 1923, *Collected Works*, vol. 33, 536.
7. Alexander Erlich, *The Soviet Industrialization Debate, 1924-28* (Cambridge: Harvard University Press, 1960), xvi.
8. Trotsky, op. cit., p. 24.
9. Lenin, *Collected Works*, vol. 33, 64.
10. Ibid., 33, 67.

Class struggle vs. economic development: rhetoric & reality

China and the 'socialist market economy'

BY IAN THOMPSON

ACCORDING to a July 2005 report in the Communist Party of China's People's Daily Online, "Minister of National Development and Reform Commission Ma Kai said [...] that China has basically completed the transition to the socialist market economy from highly centralized planning economy after 26 years' endeavor on reform."[1]

The announcement reflected the extent to which the reform program initiated by the Deng Xiaoping leadership grouping of the CPC in 1978 has shaped economic and political life in China. It also confirmed the historic defeat of the revolutionary leadership of the CPC that took place in the years up to and immediately following the death of Mao Zedong in 1976.

The struggles of overcoming colonial underdevelopment and exploitation made pulling the country from mass poverty the key task following the 1949 socialist revolution in China. From the beginning, this challenge shaped the ongoing class struggle in China, including political struggles within the CPC.

The clearest expression of the struggle was Mao and the left wing of the CPC's campaign against the "capitalist roaders" led by Liu Shaoqi and Deng Xiaoping. This "two-line struggle" emerged shortly after the 1949 revolution, but became sharpest during the Great Proletarian Cultural Revolution beginning in 1966.

The form that the struggle took varied over the years. In each case, the key issue was "politics in command"—the involvement of the working class as an agent of the revolution—versus "economics in command"—emphasizing pragmatic approaches to development and making the role of the working class secondary.

The struggle focused on which path of development to take in overcoming China's extreme underdevelopment: to develop and expand production through revolution, or to subordinate everything to economic development.

POLITICS VERSUS ECONOMICS?

The problem facing China following the 1949 revolution was described by Karl Marx in "Critique of the Gotha Programme." He said that socialism is a transitional society: "What we have to deal with here is a communist society, not as it has developed on its own foundations, but, on the contrary, just as it emerges from capitalist society; which is thus in every respect, economically, morally and intellectually, still stamped with the birth marks of the old society from whose womb it emerges."[2]

Mao and the left knew that, even under the dictatorship of the proletariat—when the political power of the capitalist class is over-thrown and replaced by a state of the working class—the massive inequalities created by capitalist rule in China could not be eliminated overnight. Inequality in wages and living conditions would continue.

Based on Marx's analysis, the left argued that it was necessary to emphasize class struggle and the political development of the Chinese masses to continue the revolution and defeat the remnants of capitalism. They understood that the economic and social relations must serve the needs of the Chinese workers and peasants.

The left noted that the revolution's survival hinged on the suc-cess of the dictatorship of the proletariat, which in turn hinged on waging class struggle against the bourgeoisie.

The right believed that China needed to integrate into the world capitalist economy in order to develop the forces of produc-tion. They ignored the primacy of continued class struggle in the transition to socialism.

Both sides in this political struggle put China's rapid economic development as a top priority.

CONSOLIDATION OF THE RIGHT

Mao died on Sept. 9, 1976. Just one month later, Deng and the right arrested Mao's allies—Jiang Qing, Zhang Chunqiao, Yao Wenyuan and Wang Hongwen, dubbed the "Gang of Four." They had helped Mao initiate the Cultural Revolution and done battle against the "capitalist roaders" within the CPC.

The Four had successfully purged Deng from the CPC's leadership in April 1976, but he continued to enjoy support from central party leaders.

The right claimed that the Four attempted to seize power. In reality, their arrest was the result of a fierce intra-party struggle. Deng played a powerful role behind the scenes.

The right launched a mass propaganda campaign against the Four, accusing them of being "anti-communist agents" and other slanders. They were blamed for the Cultural Revolution's "excesses" and were tried publicly in 1980.

Hundreds of the Four's allies in the CPC were also arrested. Over 50 of those arrested were mass leaders from the working class. One-fourth of the Central Committee was purged.

Strikes and other acts of rebellion against the suppression of the left were subdued. Left supporters among the masses had no voice within the CPC's leadership.

Deng was restored to his party leadership positions in July 1977. He led a campaign encouraging people to criticize the Cultural Revolution and its leaders.

PRO-MARKET REFORMS

Deng emerged as China's de facto leader by 1978. This led to the rapid "opening up" of China to capitalist economic markets.

Their position was pragmatic rather than Marxist. The Deng faction said that Mao had left China in a dismal economic situation. They said his policies were too ideologically motivated and not based on a scientific understanding of objective conditions. They claimed that the party's primary task "for at least 100 years" was to build the country's forces of production, which would require the introduction of market forces.

Deng argued that only market forces could ensure the technological progress necessary to build the socialist relations of production. Mao and the left wing also made rapid economic development a top priority. Between 1952 and 1976, industrial output increased annually by 11.2 percent. There was a much slower but still impressive growth in agricultural production, with a twofold increase over the same period.

Deng and those who favored the "socialist market economy," as they dubbed their scheme to privatize public property, argued that the key to China's economic development was to attract foreign capital investment from industrially advanced capitalist countries.

Mao's wing argued that although large-scale capital investment from the West and Japan would certainly develop the means of production, China would lose control of its own economy, plunging the country back into a neo-colonial status. The stronger imperialist economies would nurture a private property-owning class of capitalists in China who would ultimately take control of the state and eliminate further progress toward socialism.

> *The struggle focused on which path of development to take in overcoming China's extreme underdevelopment.*

Deng was able to put his faction's line into practice following the arrest and suppression of the left. The party began a series of far-reaching economic reforms in December 1978.

The Third Plenary Session of the 11th CPC Central Committee called for the greater use of market forces as the way to achieve a "historic shift to socialist modernization."[3]

The CPC encouraged state firms to pursue profits by granting more authority to regional planning bodies. In a speech just before the plenum, Deng said, "Under our present system of economic management, power is over-concentrated, so it is necessary to devolve some of it to the lower levels without hesitation but in a planned way."[4]

In the initial stage of reform, the CPC emphasized using centralized planning to direct economic activity and markets to create a more efficient socialist economy.

A linchpin of the plan for greater modernization was the creation of a labor market. Deng declared: "In economic policy, I think we should allow some regions and enterprises and some workers and peasants to earn more and enjoy more benefits sooner than others, in accordance with their hard work and greater contributions to society. If the standard of living of some people is raised first, this will inevitably be an impressive example to their 'neighbors,' and people in other regions and units will want to learn from them."[5]

By 1979, lifetime employment contracts were terminated. State enterprises soon were ordered to hire new workers on a contractual basis without previously guaranteed job protections.

Some state firms were allowed to sell goods above regulated government prices, causing inflation. Private enterprises began to flourish. The private sector workforce grew from 240,000 in the late 1970s to 3.4 million in 1984.

Foreign capitalist corporations were welcomed into China's "open door" in 1979. In 1980, Deng designated four economic zones open to foreign investors. Restrictions on foreign investment were relaxed.

The Chinese commune system of collectivized farms was dismantled in the early 1980s, leading to the severe stratification of the peasantry once again.

The new constitution of the People's Republic of China, adopted December 1982, enshrined the market into Chinese law. Article 15 stated, "The state practices economic planning on the basis of socialist public ownership. It ensures the proportionate and coordinated growth of the national economy through overall balancing by economic planning and the supplementary role of regulation by the market."

It transferred political and economic power from the communes to newly created township and village enterprises. Workers' rights, including basic wages, were no longer guaranteed.

At the 12th Party Congress in 1982, the party adopted the conception of a "planned commodity economy." This officially raised the status of market forces.

By 1984, the CPC shifted from planning toward greater reliance on market forces and non-state production. That year, Deng said: "Opening will not hurt us. Some of our comrades are always worried that if we open up, undesirable things may be brought into China. Above all, they worry that the country might go capitalist. ... But it will have no effect on socialism. No effect."

He continued, "The emergence of privately hired labor was quite shocking awhile back. Everybody was very worried about it. In my opinion, that problem can be set aside for a couple of years."[6]

Soon thereafter, the CPC allowed the prices of consumer and agricultural goods to move according to market forces. The four original economic zones were expanded—opening the entire coastal area to foreign investment. Deng asserted that, "Foreign investment will doubtless serve as a major supplement in the building of socialism."[7]

The CPC gave foreign investors new preferential conditions in 1986 in order to develop an export-oriented economy. China's GDP grew at an impressive pace.

Meanwhile, inflation skyrocketed as workers' income declined. Retail prices jumped more than 18 percent annually in 1988 and 1989.[8] In large urban areas, prices jumped 30 percent.

Deng launched the next stage of China's reform process in 1992. The 14th Party Congress announced its determination to establish a "socialist market economy with Chinese characteristics."

The People's Republic of China constitution was amended in 1993 to reflect this change. An updated Article 15 read: "The state has put into practice a socialist market economy. The state strengthens formulating economic laws, improves macro adjustment and control and forbids according to law any units or individuals from interfering with the social economic order."

Market reforms have increased the size of the working class and class antagonisms with the new owning class.

PHOTO: CHE CHE/COLOR CHINA PHOTO

This was a major shift. It signaled that state-owned enterprises would no longer be at the center of the Chinese economy. In the following years, nearly all small- and medium-sized state enterprises were privatized.

The CPC justified this process by arguing that private firms are more efficient. In 2002, the CPC officially allowed capitalists—in the euphemistic language of "any advanced element of other social strata"—into the party.[9]

The leadership role of the CPC in pushing these reforms cannot be understated. Its role is best spelled out in the CPC's current constitution: "The Communist Party of China leads the people in developing the socialist market economy. It unwaveringly consolidates and develops the public sector of the economy and unswervingly encourages, supports and guides the development of the non-public sector. It gives play to the basic role of market forces in allocating resources and works to set up a sound system of macroeconomic regulation."[10]

The reforms have developed over time. Each step in the process has been driven by the outlook of the CPC's leaders and the inevitable contradictions produced by the reforms themselves.

CLASS STRUGGLE IS THE KEY LINK

There appears to be little disagreement among CPC leaders about China's current economic trajectory. The party hails China's economic reforms as "important contributions to the scientific socialism theory of Marxism."[11]

The CPC continues to assert Deng's arguments in almost rote fashion, despite the nearly three decades of accumulated experience with pro-market reforms. Only economic growth figures are cited. No mention is made of the "socialist market economy's" negative impact on China's working class.

Wang Yu wrote a major article for the CPC, which was published by the Communist Party USA, titled, "Our Way: Building Socialism with Chinese Characteristics." It was intended to enlighten leftists outside China about the country's pro-market reforms.

In it, Wang re-articulates the old polemic against Mao's line of "taking class struggle as the key link." He faults the "'left'" (Mao and his allies) and says, "The task of developing the productive forces was severely neglected and people were asked to be content with poverty."

After reviewing China's historical experience, Wang states, "The CPC came to realize that although the centralized planned economy was advantageous ... it was becoming a fetter on the development of productive forces."

Wang references Marxist theory as he propounds the "theory and practice of building socialism with Chinese characteristics." He makes several points on this front:

First, that "socialism with Chinese characteristics" "defines the essence of socialism for the first time and from a scientific viewpoint." He defines the task of socialism as liberating productive forces, developing productive forces and eliminating exploitation to "achieve common prosperity."

But there is no mention of how to "achieve common prosperity" except by "liberating and developing the productive forces" and adhering to the "basic socialist principle, which retains a dominant position for public ownership and the system of distribution according to work."

This is fully consistent with the CPC's theory of "economy in command"—at the expense of politics. It postulates that economic development itself eventually will eliminate exploitation.

Wang then states, "The full development of a commodity market economy is a phase that cannot be surpassed during socialist economic development."

He also states, "The CPC has also come to realize there is no fundamental contradiction between socialism and a market economy. A market economy is indispensable to the allocation of resources in socialized production."[12]

But asserting that "socialism can coincide with a market economy"[13] negates Marx's view of the need for continuing the class struggle under the dictatorship of the proletariat.

China's "socialist market economy" is nothing more than a justification for the embrace of capitalist property relations by the CPC's leadership. There is nothing scientific about the CPC's arguments voiced by Wang.

The opening of China to transnational corporations has led to many important advances for the country's economic and technological growth. The process of urbanization, a hallmark feature of modern life, has led to an explosive growth of the industrial working class.

There are now more than 100 million factory workers in China. Cities of more than 1 million people today barely existed 20 years ago.

The Chinese government has managed increasingly to negotiate technology transfer from foreign corporations as a price they must pay to exploit the labor of Chinese workers.

Like most other oppressed countries seeking to emerge from underdevelopment, China is required to allow foreign corporations to repatriate profits back to the investors in the home country if it wants to attract capital investment. The stark alternative is a technology blockade.

Cuba too, in a much more limited way than China, opened up in the early 1990s to European and Canadian corporations, and allowed for a restrained domestic market based on private profit. As everywhere else, this led to importing much-needed capital and technology. It also immediately reproduced class stratification and the emergence of a tiny new stratum of rich people.

> *Developing the productive forces is essential, but not if it strengthens the capitalist class against the working class.*

The Cuban Communist Party, and Fidel Castro especially, called this trend by its right name. They did not proudly proclaim that they were building "socialism with Cuban characteristics." They told the truth and described these moves as a retreat away from—not toward—socialism. The collapse of the Soviet Union and its other socialist trading partners had put the Cuban economy in a downward spiral almost unmatched in present times. And as the Cuban economy recovered, they steadily, although not entirely, reversed the market reforms.

Marx defined capital as a social relationship of exploitation in the process of production. The Chinese socialist revolution broke the chains of capitalist exploitation; the ownership of the means of production was put in the hands of the workers.

But, as both Marx and Mao noted, the nationalization of property cannot by itself create a socialist society—it merely raises it as a possibility.

The existence of inequalities and differences, the vestiges of capitalism, are obstacles to the achievement of classless society. They cannot be eliminated overnight; they must be restricted and overcome.

The only way to overcome them is through public ownership in reality—not just in name.

As Mao and the CPC's left wing had warned, unless the relations of production are continually reformed and differences restricted, capitalism grows, enabling new bourgeois elements to grab more wealth and wield power over the productive process.

This reality is borne out in China today. It shines a spotlight on the CPC's erroneous "socialist market economy" rationale, and vindicates Mao's view of continuing to revolutionize society after the revolutionary triumph.

The revolutionizing of society must continue in order to defeat those who seek to preserve and widen the existent inequalities, and to combat their attempts to seize power. The class struggle is as dominant under the dictatorship of the proletariat as it was before the working class took power.

China's current leaders are correct when they say that development of the productive forces is essential. Society can only move toward communism when production moves beyond the realm of scarcity to abundance. This requires a vast expansion of the means of production.

This is what Mao was trying to do, and this is what the CPC claims it is trying to do today. Under Deng's vision, however, as the forces of production grow in China, so does the capitalist class.

Developing the productive forces is essential, but not if it strengthens the capitalist class against the working class. Increasing inequality by privatizing the economy cannot lead to the achievement of common prosperity; it can only lead to prosperity for a shrinking few.

Embracing "market forces" as the only way to build socialism does just this. It deliberately omits the essential element of class struggle from the equation and moves away from socialist planning.

The dialectical relationship between the need for economic development and the continuing class struggle negates the viability a "socialist market economy" and reveals its true nature—a way for China's national bourgeoisie to thrive under protection of the state controlled by pro-bourgeois and bourgeois forces in the CPC.

The CPC's promotion of a "socialist market economy" is a betrayal of the working class and a decisive move away from building a socialist society. But the ultimate fate of Chinese workers and their revolution has not yet been decided. □

Endnotes

1. "China has socialist market economy in place," *People's Daily Online,* July 13, 2005.
2. Karl Marx, *Critique of the Gotha Programme* (Peking: Foreign Language Press, 1972), 15.
3. Martin Hart-Landsberg and Paul Burkett, "The Slippery Slope of Market Reform: A Critical Look at the Chinese Experience," June 2, 2006.
4. Deng Xiaoping, "Emancipate the Mind, Seek the Truth from Facts and Unite as One in Looking to the Future," December 13, 1978.
5. Ibid.
6. Deng Xiaoping, "Speech at the Third Plenary Session of the Central Advisory Commission of the Communist Party of China," October 22, 1984.
7. Deng Xiaoping, "Building Socialism with a Specifically Chinese Character," June 30, 1984.
8. China's retail price index, 1977-2006, http://www.chinability.com/Prices.htm.
9. By amendment to Chapter 1 Membership, Article 1 of the Constitution of the Communist Party of China at the 16th National Congress on November 14, 2002.
10. Constitution of the Communist Party of China, amended and adopted at the 17th National Congress on October 21, 2007.
11. "China Advances with Ideological Breakthroughs," *People's Daily,* November 7, 2002.
12. Wang Yu, "Our Way: Building Socialism with Chinese Characteristics," *Political Affairs,* January 2004.
13. "China Advances with Ideological Breakthroughs," *People's Daily,* November 7, 2002.

'Precarious is China's socialism! The Chinese people have reached another extremely critical time!'

BY MA BIN, ET AL

Editor's note: On July 12, 2007, 17 members of the Communist Party of China—retired officials, military officers and academics—issued a public letter to the CPC leadership urging a reconsideration of the general line of economic reforms. It was issued on the eve of the 17th CPC Congress, which was held in October 2007.

The letter reflects the existence of a left current within the CPC that is seldom mentioned in the U.S. big-business press. The depth of support for this current is impossible to gauge from the western press.

The letter takes as its starting point the "black brick kiln" incident in the Shanxi province in northeastern China. In June 2007, Chinese state media exposed working conditions at dozens of brick kilns in the region. Children were being torn from their families to work as virtual slaves in the kiln. One manager was ultimately sentenced to death for killing a worker under his supervision. Almost 100 others, including Communist Party officials, were fired or expelled from the party as a result of the scandal.

The letter is a genuine appeal in the sense that it is written not as a general broadside, but from a point where they might be heard. They quote advocates of reform like Deng Xiaoping and current CPC General Secretary Hu Jintao, holding them to their stated allegiance to socialist development.

Their repeated calls to return to "Mao Zedong Thought" is a reference to the CPC's tradition of summarizing and acknowledging the contributions of a leadership grouping within the Party's constitution and public statements. Deng Xiaoping's contributions are known as "Deng Xiaoping Theory," Jiang Zemin's as the "Three Represents" and the 16th Congress added the "Scientific Outlook on Development." All these phrases summarize different degrees of commitment to the capitalist reforms originally launched in 1978. The letter's call for "list[ing] Marxism-Leninism Mao Zedong Thought as the Party's sole guiding ideology, rather than only airing another wave of words," is thus a veiled call for turning back the entire economic reform program.

The letter first appeared in the West in Chinese on the website www.maoflag.net. Its existence and basic contents were reported in the July 18, 2007 Los Angeles Times. The version reprinted here appeared on the website of "China Election and Governance" (www.chinaelec-tions.net) translated by Nicole Dabney, Ying Zhang and Guanhui Dai. It has been circulated on the Internet by a number of sources, including Monthly Review's mrzine.monthlyreview.org, under the title "Our Views on the Black Brick Kiln and Other Incidents and Recommendations for the 17th Party Congress." Subheads and editorial notes in square brackets have been added by Socialism and Liberation.

GENERAL Secretary Hu Jintao and the CPC Central Committee Political Bureau Standing Committee Members, Members and alternates:

In your June 25 speech at the Central Party School, you highlighted the importance of strengthening inner-party democracy, asking all party members to increase their awareness of anxieties. According to this call, we make the following recommendations.

The Shanxi black brick kiln incident has been uncovered, and some similar cases are still being discovered. For us communists, it is neither right nor possible to treat or even speak of such incidents as inevitable phenomena of the primary stage of socialism. This was obviously a capitalist scene, incorporating certain scenes of cruel exploitation and the tragic, dog-eat-dog world of primitive accumulation under feudalism and slavery. The mission of "The Communist Manifesto" and of the CPC is to eliminate exploitation and to liberate all mankind, and these incidents are totally contradictory to our philosophy.

The Shanxi black brick kiln case shows that there are many dark sides of our country that run completely counter to the socialist system and communist ideology. For example, mining accidents that have occurred constantly for years have claimed the precious lives of many good workers. The private coal mine owners take advantage of these workers to squeeze out millions and millions to fund their own luxury cars and residences—some of the large enterprises owned by the wealthiest men increase by billions every year. If these things continue to develop unhindered, will what we are building still be a socialist system? For instance, the state-owned enterprises [SOEs], which many of us have worked hard for several decades to build, have been undermined by a variety of methods, sold off or even given away for nothing, becoming what is euphemistically called collective enterprises, although they are in fact private. Former party secretaries and plant bosses become big capitalists, while continuing to act as party members and secretaries. Is this consistent with "The Communist Manifesto" and the Communist Party's founding principles? Needless to say, in the whole country, the vast majority of SOEs were also developed bit by bit through the hard work of hundreds of millions of working people under the leadership of the CPC Central Committee.

Now, the majority of property rights does not belong to the people and have become the property of private owners. Those manual workers, migrant workers, and even child labourers in the private sector, workshops, mines and shops receive low wages to do extraordinary work while others suffer the injustice of unpaid labour in dark environments. We are afraid that this is not the only instance of black brick kiln abuses, and there may be many similar cases in other places. We eliminate pornography and illegal publications every year, but it is said that millions of women are forced to engage in the cruel physical ravages of prostitution. As a result, a number of parents and children of these families suffer through life. Do we really have no way to deal with these problems; must we take a "laissez-faire" approach?

We still have a lot of large-and medium-sized state-owned enterprises that can be managed well. There is no reason to be auctioned to foreign enterprises only for them to grip our domestic market and squeeze our national economic development. The media recently reported that the state will allow foreign capital to enter the Chinese military industrial enterprises and purchase shares in joint ventures. Even if the approval was granted only for the production of ancillary equipment and parts, it is still very disturbing and should be opposed. Without reliable auxiliaries, how can we expect reliable weapons? Regardless of the weapon, it only takes one problem with parts to make normal operation impossible, and any explosion can cause fatal accidents! In addition, they will steal our intelligence, know our capabilities and encroach upon our entire military production system!

We have a number of provincial, municipal and county leaders who do not highly regard national wealth and property and will do nothing when it is cheaply sold to others. Compared to domestic private enterprises, joint ventures and wholly foreign-owned enterprises, how much of China's current GDP is produced by state-owned enterprises? Can our basic economic institution, which is underlined by public ownership, withstand the test of time? Why have state managing departments, including the Department of Statistics, not announced the statistics on proportion among different ownership sectors in the economy for many years? Workers and farmers have lost their status as masters, and the workers are either temporarily laid off or permanently unemployed with modest compensation. New land exploitation of the farmers and rich peasants, which we uprooted in the 1950s, has already begun to occur in rural areas.

In the process of economic reform, the top-down style of growing corruption, degradation of many leading cadres and betrayal of the motherland and the people runs rampant. The above issues are indeed shocking and infuriating. But every time, issues are only highlighted separately during a specific period of time. Soon after, big issues are turned into little ones and little ones turned into nothing at all. There have been very few instances where the problem is dealt with in a manner appropriate to its severity. None of the major leaders are held accountable for their actions and are dismissed or prosecuted. Only a few extremely severe cases of corruption have resulted in a few years of imprisonment, or the death penalty with reprieve at most. Corrupt officials are seldom sentenced to death. In the past, a lot of these cadres might have been good and it was only wrong ideological tendencies that caused them to betray the party and people.

There are countless concerns and troubles occurring every day, and the list goes on: bubbles in the stock market, increased prices, removal of factories without guidance, resettlement of people, speculation of real estate, soaring prices; in addition, the low-end exporting policy has led to low-wages and exploitation of workers, high energy consumption and heavy pollution, etc. More seriously, some localities defy central orders and do not report to the central government or simply ignore instructions from above. The illegal black brick kiln scandal exposed us to very serious problems regarding the future of the Party and the country, which we should now face without hesitation. This is the "cause" we are working for. Is it possible that we have digressed to the wrong road, which will lead us elsewhere?

Now, the expanding social gap has become one of the largest in the world. According to recent World Bank estimates, China's Gini index [of inequality] of 0.469 has already surpassed Britain, the United States and Japan, and even developing countries such as India, Indonesia and Egypt. Comrade Deng Xiaoping once said that if reform and opening leads to polarization, it is obvious that we are digressing. Digression is nothing but a mistake and the road of capitalism. Reform and opening have already been occurring for so many years, and yet the above social issues are only becoming more serious with development. Why do we still insist on the wrong things?

PROBLEMS ARE GROWING

On the surface, some skyscrapers have been built, along with a lot of joint ventures or foreign-owned enterprises, and state-owned enterprises have merged and expanded. But if we look past appearances to the truth, we see that the problems are growing, especially the above-mentioned dark issues. How should we respond? Can we say on the surface of the facade is the road to a better-off life? Foreign bourgeoisie and the capitalist state leaders are secretly delighted about two things: the surface of the facade and speech that sidesteps and covers conflicts. Our people see that these negative issues have not changed after all, and are anxious and fearful about the Party, country, the peoples' future and destiny, and worry that they themselves will eventually have no one or anything to depend on.

The tragedy of the Soviet Union's, and socialist Eastern European countries', collapse and the lessons from the decline of international communist movement that took place after the 1980s are still fresh in our minds. Imperialism, capitalism and their agents have encircled and suppressed us in the areas of politics, ideology, economic and political finance, educational methods, national defence and the military, diplomatic and national issues and religion. They have penetrated very deep. However, we see that the effects are not great and their measures are not effective. Although we often talk about peace, cooperation and harmony, there are indications that they are doing whatever they can to prepare the military siege against us, ready to launch a war of aggression or the threat to use force. We can currently say that the Party and government have seriously detached themselves from the people. Precarious is China's socialism! The Chinese people have reached another extremely critical time!

Faced with this kind of domestic and international situation, the majority of Party members, especially the old comrades who had received Party education for many years, are all burning with anxiety, waiting for the Central Party to take effective measures and act quickly and courageously to resolutely lead the whole party, the armed forces and the people from the "evil path," the danger of which Comrade Deng Xiaoping warned of long ago.

RETURN TO MAO ZEDONG THOUGHT

We hope in the near future it is necessary to convene the 7th Plenum of the 16th Party Congress, which should, from the black brick kiln incident as the breakthrough, summarize and reflect upon our political ideology and basic guidelines in order to, again, uphold the truth and correct the mistakes. In the 17th Party Congress we should make the decision to establish Marxism-Leninism Mao Zedong Thought as the political ideology that meets the needs of the majority of people. We sincerely recommend to the Party Central Committee that the brick kiln incidents be not excluded. We cannot talk about this issue superficially while doing nothing (the just-concluded 28th meeting of the NPC [National Party Congress] Standing Committee adopted a "Labor Contract Law," yet the media did not show the chairman, vice chairman and members of the Standing Committee of Shanxi black brick kiln incident saying a word). It should be seen as a very important breakthrough and an alarm calling for the whole Party to correct the wrong path we are on.

Chairman Mao said: "The Communist Party is the core power leading our activity and Marxism-Leninism is the guiding principle of our thought; whether our ideological and political line is correct decides everything." This is the undeniable truth. Comrade Hu Jintao said, "At any time and under any circumstances, we must always hold high the great banner of Mao Zedong Thought." This is completely correct. We fully and strongly support such reform, and eagerly look forward to implementing it practically and effectively in the future.

Our party has a glorious tradition, which is: be open and upright, do not engage in machinations; breed unity and not division; unite under the correct determination. In the interests of the people, we overcome difficulties and strive for a greater victory. Therefore, to have a fully democratic environment, the Central Committee must set an example for the entire party and create a new situation of freedom that allows party criticism of fine traditions and cadres' ability to speak their minds. The CPC Central Committee needs to listen to the majority of people, especially the workers and peasants, concentrated in line with the correct Marxist views and establish the 17th Party Congress as one which opens a correct path, achieves united victory and is of great historical significance. We must adhere to the truth without hesitation and be ready to correct mistakes, which is a very arduous task.

We should take firm action to return to the revolutionary road and list Marxism-Leninism Mao Zedong Thought as the Party's sole guiding ideology.

We recommend that we launch a study of Marxist theory before the 7th Plenum of the 16th CPC Central Committee and the 17th Party Congress. The central government should decide to select some important documents of Marxism-Leninism Mao Zedong Thought, such as: "The Communist Manifesto"; "Anti-Dühring"; "State and Revolution"; "Imperialism: the Highest Stage of Capitalism"; "Serving the People"; "Yu Gong Yi Shan"; "Study Bethune"; "Oppose Liberalism"; "Correctly Dealing with the Internal Contradictions Among the People" and other works of Chairman Mao, as well as the full lyrics of two songs, "The International" and "The Three Main Rules of Discipline and Eight Points for Attention," and have members of the Central Committee Central Commission of Discipline Inspection and representatives of the 17th Party Congress to run classes [to] seriously study. We should also organize and help all of the Party members to study as long as they have the ability to read.

We recommend that before the 7th Plenum of the 16th Party Congress of the CPC and the 17th Party Congress, we should start to criticize democratic socialism, socialist revisionism and bourgeois liberalization according to Marxism. Without abolishment, there is no establishment; without difficulty, there is no success. Without criticizing these erroneous ideas, it is impossible to truly uphold Marxism as the guiding principle and political guideline, and it would even undermine the construction of socialism. At the turn of spring and summer in 1989, because of bourgeois liberalization, a counterrevolutionary riot broke out. Comrade Deng Xiaoping pointed out that the nature of the riot was "bourgeois liberalization and opposition to 'The Four Upholdings'" (Four Basic Principles). The goal of the riot was to "subvert our country and our party." The most important lesson is that "we address the importance of the 'The Four Upholdings,' ideological and political work, anti-bourgeois liberalization and anti-spiritual pollution, but we lacked consistency, action, or did not tackle these problems adequately." He also pointed out: "In the 6th Plenum of the 16th Party Congress of the CPC, I said that we needed 20 years more to fight against bourgeois liberalization. Now it seems that it will be more than 20 years. The rampant spread of bourgeois liberalization will lead to extremely grave consequences."

Today the spread of bourgeois liberalization is greater than ever. In addition to the aggressive propaganda of bourgeois liberalization, there is another thought of bourgeois liberalization disguising itself as Marxism, and that is democratic socialism. It seriously distorts Marxist scientific socialism and denies the fundamental principles of scientific socialism—public ownership of instruments of production and dictatorship of the proletariat. It is attempting to turn China into a bourgeois country, which is the vassal of Western countries. It may confuse people because it disguises itself under the cloak of Marxism. We should seriously criticize it.

AGAINST CAPITALISTS IN THE PARTY

In short, we must thoroughly criticize all wrong anti-Marxist thinking, and establish order from this chaos to ensure the guiding status of Marxism. We suggest that the 17th Party Congress make decisions to restore the party as a vanguard of the working class, correct the wrong ideas of "dual vanguards" and change the erroneous regulation that allows capitalists to join the party. The vanguard nature of the working class has been clearly regulated since "The Communist Manifesto." As early as 1879, when the heads of the social democrats, Bernstein and others opened the doors of communist parties to the "educated, philanthropic" assets and attempted to change the Party into a "full party," Marx and Engels immediately denounced the idea and said that if they persisted in this thinking, they would have to resign or at least be removed from Party leadership positions. Since the establishment of the Communist Party of China, we have been maintaining the fundamental principle that the CPC is the vanguard of the working class. On June 9, 1952, the CPC Central Committee stressed in a document that: "All Party members would not be allowed to exploit others (regardless of whether it was feudal exploitation or capitalist exploitation). If they are reluctant to give up exploitation, or continue exploitation through kulak [rich peasant] or other forms, they should be unconditionally expelled from the party." On Sept. 16, 1956, Deng Xiaoping, on behalf of the CPC Central Committee, pointed out that: "In the report on the amendments to the Party constitution, Party members must engage in labour and not exploit the working people. We must make every Party member firmly draw a line between labour and exploitation." These fundamental principles had been maintained until the 16th Party Congress. Since the 16th Party Congress, there has been a closer relationship between the Party and bourgeoisie, but a more distant relationship between the Party and workers, peasants and working intelligentsia, and this is quite dangerous. We recommend that the 17th Party Congress restore previous regulations about the characteristics of the Party and the requirements for membership, readopting the correct Marxist stance.

For those capitalists who have already become Party members, we can give them two options: 1. Continue to be Party members by ending exploitation, returning the instruments of production currently used for exploitation to the Party and People's government and becoming labourers that depend on themselves; or 2. Automatically resign from the Party and continue to be capitalists, but love the country, obey laws and make contributions to the motherland. Some of them may join democratic parties on a voluntary basis.

A CHINESE YELTSIN?

Looking at the current facts, we have to confess that China's reform is heading towards changing public ownership to private ownership and socialism to capitalism. If the 17th Party Congress continues firmly down this path, a Yeltsin-type person will emerge, and the Party and country will tragically be destroyed very soon. However, since the specific conditions in China are different from the former Soviet Union, the Chinese version of Yeltsin may not publicly announce the dissolution of the Communist Party, change the name of the country or sell our territory. Rather, they will use Marxism-Leninism and the five-star red flag to disguise themselves and deceive the people. How did this problem begin? The answer lies in 20 years of implementing the wrong policy guided by wrong ideology.

We can summon the spirit of revolutionary struggle, work together to overcome difficulties, turn the tide, captivate the world and firmly correct the direction of socialism.

We cannot solve the fundamental problems only by adding a few social welfare policies and imprisoning some corrupt officials if we are not able to break ideological restraints, correct the privatization of the reform policy and change the wrong regulation that allow capitalists to become Party members. Without these changes, we will face endless disasters. We hope that the Central comrades in leadership can truly understand the significance of these issues.

We sincerely hope and suggest that we thoroughly deny the wrong theories and paths, thinking and approach routes to completely break away from the wrong theoretical ideas. We should take firm action to return to the revolutionary road and list Marxism-Leninism Mao Zedong Thought as the Party's sole guiding ideology, rather than only airing another wave of words. As long as we implement the above policies faithfully, all the serious problems existing in politics, theory, ideology, culture, education, economy, agriculture, industry, military, national defence, diplomacy, foreign trade, government officials, corruption and the elimination of pornography, illegal publications and gangs will be fundamentally resolved.

Faced with such a grim situation and in this extremely important historical juncture, we also recommend that the Central Standing Committee and the Politburo consider the best options, eliminate the various negative factors and overcome adversity to change the current negative situation. The CPC Central Committee Political Bureau should call on the entire party to relate the reality of China today with Marxism-Leninism Mao Zedong Thought on the proletarian revolution and proletarian dictatorship, the history of the Communist Party of China, the history of the international working-class struggle and colonial history, and study them. Leading cadres should not worry about personal gains or losses, but rather ensure that all true views of Party members can be expressed.

ORGANIZATIONAL RECOMMENDATIONS

Given the long absence of inner-Party democracy and rigid hierarchy, Party leaders have detached themselves from the people, and erroneous working styles, such as bureaucratism, sectarianism, formalism, opportunism and liberalism run rampant. Most of the people have acclimated to taking cues from the boss rather than speaking their own minds or putting forth different ideas. If this problem cannot be solved, the Party Congress and NPC will not have positive results.

Therefore, we recommend that the CPC Central Committee makes an official decision and informs the whole party that the Central Committee members, Central Commission for Discipline Inspection members, representatives of the 17th Party Congress and all of the Party members criticizing the government or putting forth different ideas should not be blamed, placed in prison, supervised or killed, and their relatives and friends must be kept safe. We must enable everyone to speak the truth. It is imperative to recall and carry forward the spirits and lessons of the Zunyi Meeting during the Long March and Yan'an Rectification Campaign in the 1940s.

Meanwhile, our Party should make a decision to welcome the retired former Party and state leaders to support the Party Congress and NPC. As for the propaganda that has been proven wrong, related comrades should, following the Party's discipline, actively avoid any restatement of these expositions and be wary of making historical mistakes. The central leaders should hold high the great banner of Marxism-Leninism Mao Zedong Thought as a guide and take the lead in conducting self-criticism. They should seek truth from facts and adopt the attitude of "speaking the truth without caring about losing face" to systematically and comprehensively summarize the experience of reform and opening in the past 30 years—what progress or error has been made and what lessons can be learned in order to uphold the truth and correct our errors. We should make policies that truthfully consider the principles of socialism and the interests of workers, peasants and the people. Regardless of how principles and policies are made or who is responsible for them, as long as they are anti-Marxist, they are inconsistent with the interests of the people previously mentioned and should be totally rejected.

The economy may be temporarily impacted, but it will gain the sincere support of the broad masses, and will therefore greatly promote political and economic unity, as well as greater development. We have friends all over the world, and we will develop.

On the issue of how to select candidates for the 17th Party Congress, we suggest that the Central Committee adheres to the principle of meritocracy. The candidates must be the ones who uphold Marxism-Leninism Mao Zedong Thought, become close to the people, contribute to peoples' interests, as well as the cause of communism, dare to maintain truth, correct mistakes, have high moral standards and ability, and be self-disciplined rather than caring too much about personal gain or loss.

We suggest that the Central Committee adjust the name list according to the situation of the 7th Plenum of the 16th Party Congress and 17th Party Congress. The decision should be made through competitive elections regulated by the Party Constitution, which was the case in the 7th Party Congress.

We suggest that the Central Standing Committee of the Political Bureau and the General Secretary be elected by all the representatives of the 17th Party Congress or the Central Committee in direct competitive elections.

TURN THE TIDE, CAPTIVATE THE WORLD!

We firmly believe that if the leading comrades of the Party Central Committee can make up their minds, realize the problems we face and truly return to the Marxist-Leninist Mao Zedong revolutionary stance without fear of pain, shame, evil or pressure, we can summon the spirit of revolutionary struggle, work together to overcome difficulties, turn the tide, captivate the world and firmly correct the direction of socialism.

We can also unite the whole Party and all the comrades who participated in the 17th Party Congress and make correct Marxist and socialist policies through study, discussion, debate and united understanding, thinking and action.

Only through the above actions can the 17th Party Congress be a successful, united and historically important one, which holds high the great banner of Marxist-Mao Zedong Thought and follows the correct path. The Chinese people and our friends from all over the world will support and praise us. The Beijing Olympic Games and Shanghai World Expo will also be successful. We will certainly be able to build a better country and the Chinese people will be able to have a better future.

Finally, let us refer to a famous poem written by Mao that stirs excitement within us all: "A cuckoo is crying in the mid-night until she throws up blood; she believes that her crying can bring the east wind back!" We deeply hope our respected leaders will stir up the east wind!

Please deeply consider the above proposals and adopt them. □

Ma Bin (former consultant, State Council Development Research Center)
Zhou Chuntian (former director, Guangxi Zhuang Autonomous Region Advisory Committee)
Li Chengrui (former director of the State Statistics Bureau)
Qin Zhongda (former minister of the Chemical Industry Ministry)
Mao Linchun (former deputy minister of the Metallurgical Industry Ministry)
Wu Fanwu (former State Department Bureau of Foreign Experts)
Yang Shouzheng (former Chinese ambassador to the Soviet Union)
Hua Guang (wife of Zhang Haifeng, former Chinese ambassador to Romania, and former minister of political affairs at the Chinese Embassy in Romania)
Han Xiya (former alternate secretary of the All-China Federation of Trade Unions)

Zang Naiguang (former deputy chief executive of the Bank of China)

Xu Chengzhi (former director of the Political Affairs Department of the PLA Railway Corps)

Long Guilin (former chief of staff of the PLA Railway Corps)

Bai Xuetian (former political commissar of a People's Liberation Army tank division)

Chen Xiao (former deputy director general of the Political Affairs Department of the PLA Navy)

Yu Quanyu (member of the CPPCC National Committee, researcher at the Chinese Academy of Social Sciences)

Xu Fei (associate professor of the Communication University of China)

Mo Mengzhe (editor, Institute of Contemporary China)

CHINA'S
REVOLUTIONARY
LEGACY

The Chinese Red Army: The making of a new kind of military

BY RICHARD BECKER

The Chinese Red Army was an exceptional organization. Led by the Communist Party of China, it was the key factor in the victory of the 1949 Chinese Revolution, which in its scope and magnitude was unparalleled in history. Established in 1927 and renamed the People's Liberation Army in 1946, the Red Army was not only a remarkable military force, but also a vital force for social change.

For a half century leading up to the triumph of the revolution, the world's most populous country was in near-constant turmoil. Tens of millions of people joined a series of mass revolts to rid the country of colonialism, feudalism and capitalism.

The 1920s saw a massive upsurge in the struggle against regional feudal warlords and the colonial powers whose "spheres of influence" left much of China under foreign rule. The 1917 Russian Revolution helped spur on the struggle—and not just by moral example.

The newly formed Soviet Union and the Communist International (Comintern) sent material assistance and advisers to both the Nationalist Party (Kuomintang, or KMT), led first by Dr. Sun Yat-sen and subsequently by Gen. Chiang Kai-shek, and to the Communist Party of China. Both organizations had explosive growth between 1925 and 1927, and had entered into an organizational alliance.

The CPC was, at the time, based among the workers and revolutionary intellectuals in the big cities, particularly Shanghai, China's main industrial city. During the 1920s, the Comintern urged the CPC to merge into the KMT and accept its leadership in the overall struggle. The result was disastrous.

In 1927, following the liberation of Shanghai and other major cities, Chiang Kai-shek's army unleashed a bloodbath against its "ally," slaughtering thousands of young communists, many in mass beheadings. The "White Terror" hunted down anyone in Shanghai suspected of being sympathetic to communism or a member of a CPC-led labor union. Chiang Kai-shek also entered into an alliance with U.S. imperialism that would last for the rest of his life.

The 1927 events, and a series of failed uprisings carrying over into 1928, reduced the CPC membership by more than 80 percent, according to Edgar Snow.[1] The party was not able to regain its former influence in the cities and industrial centers for another two decades.

The 1927 defeat presented the survivors, as members of a revolutionary Marxist workers' party, with a major dilemma: How could they hope to achieve victory and socialism deprived of a base among the industrial working class?

It was at this critical moment that Mao Zedong began to emerge as a leader of the CPC. Though one of the founding members of the party six years earlier, he was not a central leader in 1927. From a peasant background himself, Mao was assigned to rural organizing in the mid-1920s. After the stunning defeats and massacres, he began to advocate a long-term strategy based on organizing among the peasants, who comprised the vast majority of China's population, and building up a Red Army in the countryside. The Red Army was officially founded on Aug. 1, 1927, the date that Communist forces staged a rebellion, followed by a retreat, in Nanchang, Jiangxi province, about 400 miles southwest of Shanghai.

A DIFFERENT KIND OF ARMY

The Red Army was much more than just a military organization. It became the key vehicle of social transformation wherever it appeared in the vast countryside of China. There were two key elements to the CPC-led Red Army's success. First, it maintained an organic relationship with the masses of people, especially in the countryside. Second, the strategy and tactics of a new type of partisan war guided it.

At this time, the vast majority of Chinese peasants were either landless or did not have enough land to feed their families. The

The Red Army forged close ties with China's overwhelmingly peasant population, making it a genuine people's army. Here, during the Long March, 1953

conditions were declining. Big landowners, who along with China's emerging capitalist class, were the main supporters of Chiang Kai-shek and the KMT—were growing ever richer while most of the population was getting poorer.

Every drought was followed by mass flooding and locust infestations. Millions would die of starvation. Historian Lucien Bianco described the scene: "From one end of rural China to the other, ... poverty, abuse and early death were the only prospects for nearly half a billion people."[2]

The KMT army defended wealth and privilege. It was responsible for militarily repressing the peasants. In the more heavily-populated rural areas, the KMT army would, on average, sweep unannounced through the villages twice a year. All the young men and older boys would be rounded up for conscription. Those whose families could quickly raise a ransom payment would be set free—at least until the next sweep. Those who could not buy their way out were taken away in chains, and since most were illiterate, they lost touch with their families. "For his family," wrote Graham Peck, "a conscript's life usually ended on the day he disappeared down the road, shackled to his fellows."[3]

The soldier's name was then entered on the rolls of the unit so that the unit's officers could receive a food allotment for the conscript. The soldier rarely received anything like a full ration. Dying of starvation was common among soldiers, which for the commanders merely meant that they could now retain or sell the entire allotment.

Miserably paid and mistreated, KMT soldiers in turn routinely abused and plundered the population. The KMT army was so corrupt and brutal that in some regions it was more hated than the Japanese troops who occupied much of China between 1931 and 1945.[4]

The conduct of the Red Army was diametrically opposite to that of the KMT. The Red Army stood on the side of the poor, redistributed land taken from the big landlords, taught as well as fought and often worked side-by-side with the peasants.

The Red Army's conduct was based upon the "Three Rules of Discipline and the Eight Points for Attention," a code that bound all Red Army fighters. The rules—prompt obedience of orders, no confiscation of peasant property and prompt delivery to authorities of all items confiscated from landlords—were designed to contrast the Red

Army from the KMT army, as well as the warlord armies that served the big landlords.

The eight points featured such guidelines as being courteous to the people, returning any borrowed items, paying for any items taken from a home or village and being honest in all transactions with the peasants. What a contrast from the warlord armies that used to rampage through rural villages raping women, stealing property at will and then leaving the village in shambles!

It was not just the Red Army's discipline that made their army unlike any seen before in China. Where the Red Army was in command of a region, it set up a new form of government: soviets, or councils, of peasants. The Red Army helped institute land reforms and began literacy and other education programs. It worked on improving sanitation and implementing a real justice system, as opposed to the corrupt courts beholden to the landlords. The Red Army even put on plays and other entertainment in areas that it governed.

These decisive factors won over tens of millions of people to the side of the revolution.

In 1936, Edgar Snow became the first Western journalist to interview Mao and travel with the Red Army. In his classic "Red Star Over China," he described a conversation with two teenaged Red Army fighters. When he asked them if they liked the Red Army, Snow says they looked at him "in genuine amazement."

"The Red Army has taught me to read and to write," replied one of the two, who was 17. "Here I learned how to operate a radio, and how to aim a rifle straight. The Red Army helps the poor."

"It is good to us and we are never beaten," said his 16-year-old comrade. "Here everybody is the same. It is not like the White districts [under KMT control], where poor people are slaves of the landlords and the Kuomintang. ... Why should anyone not like an army such as this?"[5]

Countless similar reports came from Snow and journalists who arrived after him.

NEW STRATEGY AND TACTICS

The other key factor in the victory of the revolution was the new war doctrine adopted by the CPC and the Red Army. Mao elaborated four general guidelines for partisan warfare—people's war fought against an enemy with superior numbers, equipment and funds.

The Red Army followed a strategy based on Mao's well-known words articulating these guildelines: "The enemy advances, we retreat; the enemy camps, we harass; the enemy tires, we attack; the enemy retreats, we pursue."

The Red Army would try to avoid any battle that it would lose. This might sound simplistic; no army wants to lose any battles. What Mao and the other military commanders—Peng Dehuai, Lin Biao, Liu Bocheng and others—meant was to refuse to join battle unless they were nearly assured of victory. This was not always possible, of course. At times, they were forced into battle. But, in general, the Red Army commanders sought to conserve and build their forces and avoid the type of positional warfare where two opposing armies would meet head-on on a battlefield—until they were strong enough to do so successfully.

During the war against Japan, the rival Chinese armies both grew in number. The Red Army grew from over 100,000 fighters in 1940 to around 1 million by the end of the war in 1945. The KMT army, which spent far more time and energy fighting the Red Army than the Japanese occupiers, grew based on greater U.S. supplies of gold and arms.

But while it grew in numbers, the KMT did not become a stronger fighting force. Even U.S. generals in China during and after World War II, while unquestionably anti-communist, had contempt for the corrupt and ineffectual KMT army.

After the war ended, the CPC refused to agree to Chiang's demand to disarm and accept a subordinate position. The civil war resumed.

Between September 1948 and January 1949, the tide turned decisively. In two huge campaigns—one in Manchuria and the other known as the Hwai-hai campaign further south—the KMT army lost over 1 million men to defections, capture and casualties. Many went over to the Red Army entire divisions at a time, taking their U.S.-supplied equipment.

At the beginning of 1949, the Red Army, vastly outnumbered just a few years before, now had superiority even in that category. Beijing, Shanghai and Tianjin, the largest cities of north and central China, all fell without a battle. The scale of the decisive battles showed that the Red Army—now the People's Liberation Army—was not a peasant army in any traditional sense. It had developed into a highly sophisticated military machine.

On Oct. 1, 1949, Mao Zedong announced the establishment of the People's Republic of China before a huge crowd in Tiananmen Square, proclaiming the famous words "China has stood up." The old state of the Kuomintang had collapsed. The new state, based on the People's Liberation Army, was being constructed. ☐

Endnotes

1 Edgar Snow, *Red Star Over China* (New York: Grove Press, 1938), 22.

2 Lucien Bianco, *Origins of the Chinese Revolution*, 1915-1949, trans. Muriel Bell (Stanford, Calif.: Stanford University Press, 1971), 87.

3 Graham Peck, *Two Kinds of Time* (Boston: Houghton-Mifflin, 1950), 226, quoted in Lucien Bianco, *Origins of the Chinese Revolution*, 156.

4 Lucien Bianco, *Origins of the Chinese Revolution*, 156.

5 Edgar Snow, *Red Star Over China*, 83.

The contributions of Mao Zedong

BY CARLITO ROVIRA

THROUGHOUT the 1950s, the question asked in U.S. ruling circles was, "Who lost China?" Their imperial arrogance could not fathom that hundreds of millions of oppressed Chinese peasants and workers could free themselves from the bondage of imperialism and colonialism.

The person who was most hated by the imperialists in those years was Mao Zedong, the most prominent leader of the Chinese Revolution. It was exactly because he embodied the aspirations and class instincts of the peasants and workers that the owning class so despised him. That was so while he was still alive, and it remains so today.

Mao Zedong was born on Dec. 26, 1893, to a relatively well-to-do peasant family in the village of Shaoshan, China. He was an exemplary and dynamic youth, always eager to learn. As a result of his father's encouragement, Mao was attracted to academic studies.

Mao grew up at a time when China's class struggle was completely enmeshed within the international situation of imperialist competition and war. Since the middle of the 19th century, all the imperialist countries were competing for influence and plunder in China.

A new wave of European religious missionaries arrived in China at the beginning of the 19th century to accomplish this end. Despite this, the mood of rebellion was so widespread among the peasants that Chinese converts to Christianity organized the Taiping Rebellion. It was the largest and longest peasant rebellion in China's history, lasting from 1850 to 1864. The peasant rebels created the "Taiping Heavenly Kingdom," where no representative from western Christian churches was allowed to influence the "Heavenly government."[1]

Europe's intensifying intrusion into Chinese society sparked the Boxer Rebellion of 1899 to 1901. That uprising was only put down with an expeditionary force of 50,000 combined troops from Japan, Russia, Britain, France and the United States.

China is a country with 56 ethnic groups that speak many languages. It is a territory that stretches about 3,100 miles from east to west, and about 3,400 miles from north to south, with a contrast of varying terrains and climates. Most of China's population prior to the 1949 revolution was illiterate peasants. To lead a revolution in a country facing such a low level of development required the highest level of understanding of the complexities of the people.

SWEPT INTO REVOLUTION

When Mao was 18 years old, revolution swept through China. The nationalist movement led by Sun Yat-sen toppled the old Qing Dynasty in October 1911, which by that point was little more than a puppet for Western imperialist interests. Mao Zedong joined a regiment that fought on the side of the democratic revolution to overthrow the monarchical rule of the Qing Dynasty. It was where he got his first experience in military affairs—an area to which he would contribute greatly in his revolutionary career.

At the end of his schooling from the First Provincial Normal School of Hunan in 1918, Mao traveled to Beijing with his mentor, high school teacher and future father-in-law, Yang Changji. Yang arranged for Mao to work part-time and attend classes at the Beijing University. Here Mao became exposed to Marxism—which was gaining the attention of many in the oppressed world after the 1917 Russian Revolution.

In Beijing, he came in contact with the anti-imperialist May Fourth Movement, which conducted demonstrations in 1919 to denounce the encroachments of the Western powers.

On July 23, 1921, Mao went to Shanghai to attend the founding congress of the Communist Party of China. "At that time there were in the whole of China 57 Marxists," wrote Mao biographer Han Suyin.[2] Following the meeting, he returned to Hunan where he set up both workers' organizations and the regional party branch. He lived with coal miners in Anyuan, setting up workers' study groups and leading a number of strikes over the next several years.

During this early period after the founding of the CPC, one of the main questions facing the communists was their relationship with the Kuomintang (KMT)—a mass nationalist party led by Sun Yat-sen.

By 1923, the CPC pursued a policy of a united front with the KMT. Mao was designated as a liaison between the two parties.

Starting in 1925, he began the work he would become most renowned for—organizing the peasants. He began a series of surveys, going from house to house and village to village, collecting data and organizing as he went. Many of the results of those investigations became the basis for Mao's first major works, "Analysis of Classes in Chinese Society" (1926) and "Report on an Investigation of the Peasant Movement in Hunan" (1927). His study and orientation ultimately enabled the Communist Party of China to draw the necessary strategy and tactics to win this oppressed class to the side of a socialist revolution.

THE FIRST REVOLUTION

During 1926 and 1927, the Kuomintang and the Communist Party were in a fragile alliance to launch a joint military venture known as the Northern Expedition. It set out to destroy the armies of feudal warlords and to guard against the threat posed by Japanese ambition.

Sun Yat-sen had died in 1925. The KMT had many different political currents. A left wing in the Kuomintang was more nationalistic and wanted to pave the way for the development of indigenous capitalism without feudal or foreign interference. There was also a right wing, closely tied with the big landowners, which feared communism more than Japanese imperialism and resented the CPC's influence within the KMT. In 1926, Chiang Kai-shek took over the party's leadership. Although Chiang had been a non-communist representative to the Soviet-based Communist International in the early 1920s, he emerged in 1927 as the leader of the most right-wing and viciously anti-communist wing of the KMT.

In 1927, tensions between the two parties exploded. Revolutionary strikes and peasant uprisings spread in major cities like Shanghai. Fearing the growing workers' and peasants' movement, Chiang Kai-shek unleashed a wave of counterrevolutionary violence, killing tens of thousands of communist-led workers. The CPC, which had grown to close to 58,000 members in just six years,[3] was under the political influence of the Communist International. Having been unexpectedly routed by its KMT allies in Shanghai, the CPC tried to stage a workers' uprising in Guangdong later in 1927. This uprising was an ill-prepared reflex to the defeat in Shanghai. It prompted another murderous wave of repression by the KMT government.

While the party's base in the cities was being smashed, a political struggle erupted in the summits of the CPC.

"I was very dissatisfied with the party policy then," Mao said. "I think that if the peasant movement had been more thoroughly organized and armed for a class struggle against the landlords, the soviets would have had an earlier and far more powerful development throughout the whole country."[4]

During the years of repression that followed, Mao's wife Yang Kaihui and their eight-year-old-son, Mao Anying, were arrested by the Kuomintang. KMT soldiers forced the young Anying to watch his mother tortured and killed. This deep personal tragedy undoubtedly added to Mao Zedong's determination to overthrow the brutal Kuomintang.

LIBERATED ZONES IN THE COUNTRYSIDE

The Communist Party was on the defensive in the late 1920s and early 1930s. While some communist leaders mistakenly believed they were able to challenge Chiang Kai-shek's advancing forces, Mao Zedong advised against engaging the Kuomintang in conventional warfare and repeatedly urged for a tactical retreat.

Mao organized the remnants of the communist forces in the countryside of the Jiangxi region south of Shanghai. In 1931, the region was declared the "Chinese Soviet Republic." The population was armed to defend itself against Chiang's military attacks.

By 1933, however, Mao understood that a stationary base could not hold out against encirclement and repeated attacks. In October 1934, Mao, as commander of the First Red Army, led a massive effort that became known as the Long March. The organized military retreat involved more than 100,000 people. There were tens of thousands of combatants along with an even larger number of peasant families who would have been slaughtered as "communist sympathizers" by the advancing KMT armies. This downtrodden mass of humanity was organized to march thousands of miles taking only what they could carry on their backs.

The retreat lasted over a year and covered a distance of 5,965 miles from Jiangxi province in the southeast to Shaanxi province in the central north. They crossed mountain ranges and forded rivers with no bridges while being attacked by a better-armed enemy. More than half of those who started the march perished along the way in clashes with enemy forces and from the harsh conditions in difficult terrain and weather.

Amid the hardships, the retreating forces won the support of the Chinese peasant masses. Red Army units came to the luxurious dwellings of wealthy landlords and arrested them. Revolutionaries seized the landlords' hoarded resources—crops, livestock, clothing, medicines and weapons. The resources were distributed among the impoverished, starving peasants along the path of the Long March, and also allowed the Red Army to sustain itself. Instead of plundering and pillaging as they went, the new people's army paid for their food. The Chinese peasants had never experienced such an armed force.

Mao Zedong's First Red Army finally reached its destination in Shaanxi province in October 1935 and met up with the Second Red Army and remnants of the Fourth Red Army. The Chinese revolution was saved with its organizational nucleus intact.

Mao Zedong, 6th plenary session of the 6th Central Committee, Yenan, 1938

THE LIBERATION WAR

In 1937 Japan invaded China as part of its effort to recolonize the continent. As in 1925, the CPC offered a united front with the Kuomintang to fight the Japanese invasion. The difference this time was that the communist Red Army was a powerful and battle-tested force with the confidence of millions of peasants.

The Communist International insisted that the Red Army be disbanded as an independent force and merged under the command of the KMT. This had been the demand of the bourgeois nationalist leadership of Chiang Kai-shek. Mao agreed to change the name of the army to the 8th Route Army of the KMT, but in reality the communists never relinquished control over their command structure.

Without having retained independent control over its armed forces, the final victory by the Communist Party of China in the civil war of 1945 to 1949 would have been impossible. Unlike many of the communist parties in the west, Mao's leadership was noteworthy for its independence from the Soviet leadership. It maintained a relationship of solidarity with the Soviet Union and it recognized the centrality of its leadership in the world communist movement—but the Chinese Revolution was successful because it did not follow every instruction of the Soviet party.

Throughout World War II, Chiang Kai-shek proved to be an unreliable opponent of the Japanese imperialists, preferring to stage military actions against the Red Army. The Communists, on the other hand, won the respect of the nation as the true anti-imperialist forces. The mass base of the Chinese revolution made it unpleasant for the Japanese invaders, who had to contend with the skillfulness of Red Army guerrilla units.

After Japan's defeat in World War II, the civil war resumed. It was a period of dual power in China. Mao Zedong and the CPC had gained the respect and admiration of the Chinese people, while the government, now in the hands of the KMT, stood discredited with its military troops demoralized. From his base area in Yan'an, Mao Zedong called for intensifying efforts to overthrow the Chiang Kai-shek government.

In 1949, the People's Liberation Army marched into Beijing. On Oct. 1, 1949, Mao Zedong proclaimed the Peoples' Republic of China, opening his famous declaration by stating, "The Chinese people have stood up."

In the city of Chengdu on Dec. 10, 1949, the last holdout of Kuomintang soldiers surrendered to the Red Army. Chiang Kai-shek had already fled to the Chinese island province of Taiwan.

ANTI-COMMUNIST FRENZY

Bourgeois circles throughout the imperialist world were in a frenzy during this period. The Soviet Union had broken the U.S. monopoly on atomic weapons. Socialism had expanded to half the European continent. National liberation struggles ignited in the colonized regions throughout the world. Challenges to the racist Jim Crow system in the United States were mounting.

Nothing alarmed the U.S. capitalist class more than "losing China," however. Not since the 1917 Russian Revolution had the international situation been so impacted by such a victory.

In every capitalist state, anti-communist propaganda intensified to the point of hysteria. The mass media vilified Mao Zedong in order to demonize the Chinese revolution. Senator Joseph McCarthy initiated anti-Communist witch-hunts aimed at stifling the growth of a revolutionary movement in the United States.

Although the U.S. government attempted to do everything it could to isolate the Chinese Revolution, people all over the world were drawn to it out of objective class commonalities. The rise of liberation movements in Africa, Asia and Latin America as well as the U.S. Civil Rights Movement instinctively favored a beacon of defiance in the international realm.

INSPIRATION FOR NEW REVOLUTIONARIES

The Peoples' Republic of China defied imperialism. Beijing supported the national liberation movements on all continents—in many cases providing material aid. Mao reached out to the militant struggles of African Americans and other oppressed peoples in the United States. It was a breath of fresh air at a time when the Soviet Union's leadership was in the midst of its long-time policy of non-revolutionary appeasement towards U.S. imperialism.

For those who became disillusioned with the Soviet Union and wished to bring back the militancy of the international communist movement, the Chinese Revolution provided hope. Many around the world were inspired to engage in efforts for the creation of a new movement and re-examine the possibilities of making revolution in the United States.

The Chinese Revolution took place far away from the European context where the original socialist revolutions had been expected to happen. It became a factor that enhanced the relevance of Marxism-Leninism to Black and Latino revolutionaries in the United States as well as for the national liberation struggles in the traditionally colonized regions of the world. No longer could scientific socialism be derided as a "European ideology."

Political organizations of oppressed peoples like the Black Panther Party, the Young Lords and the Brown Berets openly proclaimed themselves communists—thanks in large part to the Chinese Revolution. Many of these groups based their political education on the "Red Book"—"Quotations of Chairman Mao Zedong."

It was only after Mao invited Nixon to China in 1972 and resumed relations with the United States on the basis of an anti-Soviet alliance did China back away from its historic commitment to the national liberation movements. This signaled the beginning of the end of the heroic era of the Chinese Revolution. It badly tarnished China's revolutionary credentials and led to a global collapse of the hundreds of political parties that had earlier associated with Maoism based on it being a beacon light for true fighters against imperialism.

Despite this later turn, Mao Zedong's contributions to the struggle for socialism during his lifetime continue to provide lessons for revolutionaries today. His leadership in facing the tremendous task of making a revolution in the world's most populous country is an example that nothing can stop a determined people from taking control of their own destiny—once they have a steeled organization capable of leading that struggle. This is precisely why Mao Zedong became the embodiment of the Chinese Revolution. □

Endnotes

1. H. Ouanyu, Ch. Tong, and R. Ountz, "Marxism and Christianity Within the Great Wall," *Asian Philosophy* vol. 4 no. 1, 1994.
2. Han Suyin, *The Morning Deluge: Mao Tse-tung and the Chinese Revolution* (Little, Brown), 1972.
3. Ibid., 154.
4. Ibid., 156.

The Sino-Soviet split

From revolutionary potential to tragic consequences

BY MONICA RUÍZ

THE year 1969 was one of the high points in the world revolutionary movement. The Vietnamese Revolution was gaining momentum in its fight against U.S. imperialism. The Black liberation movement was sweeping the United States, propelling forward the anti-war and other national liberation struggles. People's struggles were sweeping every continent.

But 1969 also witnessed one of the lowest points in the history of the workers' movement. In March 1969, troops from the two most powerful socialist countries, the Soviet Union and China, clashed across the Ussuri River border.

The firefights between troops of two former allies marked the sharpest point in what is known as the Sino-Soviet split. While all-out war was averted, the impact of that split reverberated for decades. It culminated in a strategic alliance between U.S. imperialism and China against the Soviet Union, an alliance that damaged the world-wide working class and strengthened imperialism precisely at a time when it was weakest.

What caused the bitter split between the Union of Soviet Socialist Republics and the People's Republic of China? How did the ideological dispute between the two most prestigious communist parties spiral downward to a conflict between states that were each trying to build socialism?

REVOLUTION IN RUSSIA AND CHINA

The Russian Revolution took place in 1917 after more than three years of czarist Russia's involvement in World War I. Three years of civil war and imperialist intervention followed the revolution. Then, with barely over 20 years of peace, the Soviet Union faced invasion by the most powerful military yet created—the German Nazi war machine. By 1945, 27 million Soviet workers and peasants had been killed in the war, and around two-thirds of the country's industry had been destroyed.

The Chinese Communists, by comparison, achieved power in 1949 after more than 20 years of civil war and resistance to Japanese imperialist invasion and occupation. When the People's Republic of China was declared on Oct. 1, 1949, it not only brought an end to over two decades of war, but also to what was called the "century of humiliation" as a result of colonialist brutality and exploitation at the hands of the world imperialist powers. Yet, within a year, one million Chinese People's Volunteer Army troops heroically came to the aid of the Korean Revolution following the U.S. invasion of Korea in 1950.

Both China and the Soviet Union desperately needed peace. No countries had suffered more from imperialist war. The basis of their agreements and disagreements in the following decades revolved around the question of how to win peace in the face of an extremely aggressive, nuclear-armed U.S. imperialism.

SINO-SOVIET COOPERATION

Just months after the triumph of the Chinese Revolution, Communist Party of China leader Mao Zedong traveled to Moscow, later joined by Foreign Minister and Premier Zhou Enlai and a large Chinese delegation. In February 1950, after six weeks of discussions, the two states signed the historic "Sino-Soviet Treaty of Friendship, Alliance and Mutual Assistance."

Despite the fact that the treaty was between two states committed to building socialism (though China did not explicitly say so until a few years later), the signing of the treaty was neither automatic nor easy. There was a tension between proletarian internationalism, the guiding principle of communist foreign policy since the time of Marx and Engels, and the perceived national interests of the respective ruling parties. That tension was far more tenacious than earlier Marxist leaders could have imagined.

There had been a number of conflicts between the leaders of the Soviet Union and China before the triumph of the Chinese

Revolution. A long-standing source of tension was the Soviet leadership's relationship with Chiang Kai-shek, leader of the Nationalist Party (Kuomintang, or KMT), the U.S.-backed capitalist party that ruled China until overthrown in 1949. After World War II, Soviet Prime Minister Joseph Stalin, apparently not having the confidence that the CPC and its army could win a civil war, had urged the Chinese communists to become junior partners in a post-war KMT government.[1]

Stalin had urged the CPC to take the same course in the 1920s. That period ended in the mass slaughter and near-annihilation of the young party at the hands of Chiang in 1927. The second time around, Mao and the CPC agreed in words but did not disband the communist-led Red Army. No real coalition government was ever set up after World War II. Instead, the CPC forces smashed the huge but corrupt and demoralized forces of the KMT in 1948 and 1949.

The 1950 treaty and other agreements reached at the time between the Soviet Union and China pledged mutual defense, the withdrawal of Soviet forces from bases in Manchuria that had been occupied after the Japanese defeat, the provision of long-term credits and the aid of Soviet experts in building and renovating 50 key Chinese industrial establishments and military bases.

In 1953, when China initiated its first Five-Year Plan, the USSR greatly expanded economic assistance, including new factories and rail lines.[2] The importance of this aid to China, an overwhelmingly rural country struggling to overcome the devastation left by war and colonialism, cannot be overstated.

The following year, Nikita Khrushchev, the new first secretary of the Communist Party of the Soviet Union after Stalin's death in March 1953, announced another expansion of assistance and mutual aid, including the building of two new railways to link the two countries.

In 1955, the two states reached an agreement on nuclear cooperation. The Soviet Union was to provide expertise, aid and materials to enable China to develop nuclear power.

Facing nuclear-armed U.S. submarines and surface ships, and U.S. bases in Japan and other nearby countries, it was hardly surprising that China was seeking to develop nuclear weapons as well as nuclear power. At the same time, Foreign Minister Zhou Enlai repeatedly stated China's call for the total prohibition of nuclear weapons and universal disarmament—something that all U.S. leaders have refused to even discuss.

Against this backdrop of growing cooperation, a leadership struggle was taking place within the CPSU between 1953, the year of Stalin's death, and 1956, when Khrushchev emerged as the pre-eminent leader.

KHRUSHCHEV'S 1956 SPEECH

In February 1956, Khrushchev gave his "secret speech" to the 20th Congress of the CPSU. In the course of the speech, he made a lengthy criticism of Stalin and his policies. He also announced new policies that amounted to a sharp rightward shift.

Khrushchev outlined two key revisions to fundamental Marxist views on war and revolution. First, according to Khrushchev's new theory, imperialist war was no longer inevitable. The military strength of the socialist camp, including the Soviet Union's possession of nuclear bombs, could deter imperialism's natural tendency toward war. Second, he announced that it was now possible, given the shift in world politics, to achieve socialism without revolution—that there was what was often called a "parliamentary road to socialism."

Khrushchev soon after began to promote what he termed "non-capitalist development." Through economic alliance with the Soviet Union and other socialist states, the national bourgeoisie or "patriotic capitalist class" in formerly colonized countries could now advance toward socialism. For this reason, he argued, communist parties in the oppressed countries should support these national bourgeois forces.

All of these issues, including the role of Stalin, were to become the subjects of sharp disputes within a few years. But at the time of the speech, the CPC endorsed and supported Khrushchev's report.

The Khrushchev report led to upheavals within many communist parties. That turmoil helped trigger a counterrevolutionary revolt in Hungary in October 1956. The CPC supported the intervention of Soviet troops in Hungary to prevent the restoration of capitalism.

DIFFERENCES EMERGE

While economic cooperation and Soviet aid continued, differences between the CPSU and CPC began to emerge in 1959 and 1960.

In June 1959, the Soviet Union repudiated a secret agreement to assist China in developing nuclear weapons.

Three months later, Khrushchev visited the United States to hold three days of private talks with President Dwight D. Eisenhower. Khrushchev highly praised Eisenhower, saying that the U.S. president "sincerely wants to liquidate the cold war and improve relations between our two great countries."[3] This was at the time of the "Eisenhower Doctrine," the foreign policy proclaimed in January 1957, which stated the U.S. government's intention to send troops to prevent the alleged spread of communism in the Middle East.

The U.S.-Soviet summit meeting marked a turning point for Sino-Soviet relations. China felt snubbed. It feared that Khrushchev might be negotiating over a tense border standoff between China and Soviet ally India. Khrushchev's follow-up visit to Beijing eased no fears, with the Soviet leader displaying a chauvinist attitude toward his Chinese hosts.[4]

Open differences emerged in April 1960. The Chinese published a series of articles titled "Long Live Leninism." While agreeing that communists should seek to prevent a major war, the articles argued that such a war was likely as long as capitalism and imperialism existed. It also quoted Lenin's view that the transition to socialism was not possible without revolution, and advocated the support of revolutionary movements "without the slightest reservation."

"Long Live Leninism," "The Differences Between Comrade Togliatti and Us" and many similar publications electrified the world communist movement, and particularly millions of students and young workers who came into political life during the 1960s. Revolutionary China had tremendous prestige and that prestige lent great weight to the views of its leaders. The CPC's publications, printed in many languages and distributed at very low cost, played an irreplaceable role in reviving revolutionary Marxism on a world scale.

The CPSU responded by attacking "dogmatism" and "outmoded ideas," arguing that imperialist war was no longer inevitable and that the growing strength of the socialist camp could lead to the worldwide triumph of socialism without war. "One cannot mechanically repeat now on this question," stated Khrushchev, "what Lenin said many decades ago on imperialism."[5]

On July 16, 1960, the Soviet government sent a letter informing the Chinese government that it was withdrawing all Soviet technicians and canceling more than 600 technical aid and scientific contracts and projects. Blueprints and plans were taken as well.[6]

This unilateral act was a devastating blow to China's economy. It came at a time of natural disasters, which China's national radio said were "without parallel in the past century," and included plagues of locusts, extreme flooding and widespread drought.[7]

The cancellation of all economic aid was intended to punish the Chinese leadership. It caused severe harm to the economy and population and greatly embittered the relations between the two states by extending the ideological struggle into the area of state-to-state relations.

> *The perceived national interests of the leaders of both states overwhelmed working-class internationalism, to the advantage of imperialism and detriment of the world struggle.*

Another point of contention between the Chinese and the Soviets was Khrushchev's signing of a partial nuclear test ban treaty with the United States and Britain in 1963. The Chinese, who had been excluded from the meetings, denounced the deal as "a dirty fraud" and an attempt by the three states to maintain a nuclear monopoly.[8] At the time, U.S. hostility and provocations against China were sharply escalating. Both the massive U.S. intervention in Vietnam starting in 1964 and the 1965 coup and massacre of over a million members of the pro-CPC Indonesian Communist Party were aimed at China as well as those countries directly affected.

Despite the deepening rift, China and the Soviet Union did not differ on all points, nor did they break off diplomatic relations. Both countries supported the 1959 Cuban Revolution. Both gave vital aid to Vietnam. The Soviet Union continued to advocate that China be given a seat in the United Nations. Trade continued between the two countries, although at reduced levels.

But for all practical purposes—military, political, diplomatic and economic—China was now outside of the socialist camp.

In a world divided into two major class camps, this posed a grave danger, which at the time still seemed unthinkable. Was it possible for China to stay outside of the life-and-death struggle between U.S. imperialism and the Soviet Union? Or would China become drawn into allying itself with U.S. imperialism against the Soviet Union?

FROM 'REVISIONISM' TO 'SOCIAL IMPERIALISM'

By 1966, the ideological struggle had been transformed into a state-to-state conflict on both sides. The CPC accusations that the CPSU was "revisionist"—that is, revising Lenin's positions on imperialism, war and revolution—escalated to charges that the Soviet Union was "fascist" in February 1967 and that it had restored capitalism by May 1968. In August 1968, after the Warsaw Pact intervention in Czechoslovakia to halt the restoration of capitalism there, Chinese leaders began calling the Soviet Union "social imperialist."

There was no objective evidence for the allegation that the USSR had somehow become capitalist, much less imperialist or fascist. There was no sign of the dismantling of the socialized core of the economy.

With the start of the Cultural Revolution in August 1966, the hostility further deepened. Demonstrations outside the Soviet embassy in Beijing involved assaults on Soviet personnel. In January 1967, Leonid Brezhnev, then general secretary of the CPSU, denounced the Cultural Revolution, calling it "a tragedy for all true Chinese Communists."[9]

Mutual charges led to greatly heightened tensions along the long border separating the two countries. In 1968 and 1969, there were numerous clashes, some involving casualties. More than 600,000 troops from both sides were concentrated on the border regions. Both sides, fortunately, pulled back from the abyss of what would have been a truly senseless war between states.

Just as there was no guarantee that the Union of Soviet Socialist Republics and People's Republic of China could achieve unity in 1950, there was nothing automatic or predestined about the split between the two countries just a few years later.

The ideological struggle by the CPC against Soviet revisionism focused on the issue of how best to wage the struggle against imperialism that made an invaluable contribution to the revival of revolutionary Marxism and Leninism.

Unfortunately, the degeneration of the debate became a material factor in the class struggle both in China and the world. The perceived national interests of the leaders of both states overwhelmed working-class internationalism, to the advantage of imperialism and detriment of the world struggle. It is a lesson for future revolutionary leaders to study and learn from. □

Endnotes

1. Han Suyin, *The Morning Deluge: Mao Tse-tung and the Chinese Revolution* (Little, Brown, 1972), 504.
2. Bill Brugger, *China, Liberation and Transformation, 1942-62* (London: Croom Helm; Totowa, N.J., 1981), 89.
3. "The Sino-Soviet Dispute," *Keesing's Research Report*, (New York: Charles Scribner's Sons, 1969), 20.
4. 'When masters quarrel, the servants are shaking in their shoes' is a phrase that escaped Khrushchev when he referred to 'the two greatest states in the world, on whom depend war and peace.'—presumably referring to the United States and the Soviet Union. Han Suyin, *Wind in the Tower* (Jonathan Cape, 1976), 167-69.
5. "The Sino-Soviet Dispute," 28.
6. Ibid., 29.
7. Ibid.
8. Ibid., 59.
9. Ibid., 95.

From liberation to Thermidor

Phases of China's socialist revolution

BY EUGENE PURYEAR

REVOLUTIONS are traditionally marked by the year that the old state is defeated: the 1789 French Revolution, the 1917 Russian Revolution or the 1949 Chinese Revolution, for example. In each of these great social upheavals, the old ruling-class state was defeated and a state representing a new social class was built.

The final conquest of political power is a single historical moment, but a social revolution is a profound transformation that does not take place over weeks or months, but years—a reality this tradition fails to take into account. The defeat of the old ruling-class state opens the door for the economic, political and cultural changes that meet the needs of the new class in power. In the case of a socialist revolution, that means changes that safeguard the interests of the working class, small farmers and other oppressed sectors.

That was certainly the case in China. The 1949 revolution took place in a country still containing elements of feudal relations. Most Chinese people were peasants, not workers. Landlords exploited millions who worked the land, despite land reforms carried out in territories liberated by the Red Army.

Economist Arthur G. Ashbrook, Jr., described China—the world's most populous country—as it existed in 1949:

> Since the fall of the Manchu Dynasty in 1911, extensive areas of China had been wracked by revolution, warlordism, civil war, foreign invasion, and flood and famine. ... Dams, irrigation systems and canals were in a state of disrepair. Railroad lines had been cut and recut by contending armies. ... Finally, the population had suffered enormous casualties from both man-made

and natural disasters and was disorganized, half starved and exhausted.[1]

For this reason, one of the immediate tasks of the Chinese Revolution was to rapidly develop the economy. Industries belonging to counterrevolutionaries who had abandoned their property and fled the mainland, as well as many foreign companies that had been given special privileges in capitalist China, were nationalized.

Land reform, the most pressing demand for the vast majority of China's population, was approached gradually. Large estates were broken up into smaller holdings and turned over to the peasants who worked them. Collective approaches to agriculture were set up slowly and in a skeletal form.

Between 1952 and 1955, private capital was essentially eliminated in China. Socialist planning was instituted for economic production and distribution, and the state established a monopoly of foreign trade.

Under the slogan "Learn from the Soviet Union," the Communist Party of China approached the economy based on the model developed by Soviet economists. Heavy industry was given priority, with over half of all investment going to capital goods industries. Planning in consumer goods industries was more decentralized than in the Soviet Union, with regional planning authorities having a wider purview.

Through their own efforts and with significant technical assistance from the Soviets, the gross output value of all industry increased by 128 percent during the first Five-Year Plan from 1953 to 1957, according to official figures. The agricultural sector only received 6.2 percent of the budget, but still managed to increase the gross output value by 24.7 percent.[2]

All of this economic growth took place alongside massive state investment in social services. The state instituted a public health program that was able to eliminate typhoid, plague and cholera. Educational programs were greatly expanded, including a major campaign to end illiteracy that involved fifty million peasants in 1952 and 1953.[3]

DEEPENING THE REVOLUTION

Following the initial phase of the revolution, the Communist Party of China set out in 1957 to strengthen socialist approaches to development. The Central Committee described the new course in November 1957:

> To carry out the technological and cultural revolu-
> tion simultaneously with the socialist revolution on the
> political and ideological fronts; to develop industry and
> agriculture simultaneously with priority development of
> heavy industry; to develop central and local industries
> simultaneously under central leadership, overall plan-
> ning and in coordination; and to develop large, medium
> and small enterprises simultaneously. To build socialism,
> faster, better and more economically by exerting efforts to
> the utmost and pressing ahead consistently.[4]

In January 1958, the second Five-Year Plan—known as the "Great Leap Forward"—began.[5]

The core of the initiatives was the introduction of socialist mea-sures in the countryside—the "commune" system. For the first decade following the revolution, there was some collectivization, but on a much smaller scale. These communes were essentially entire rural vil-lages that pooled together resources and labor and functioned as the basic unit of both the economy and the government. They involved thousands or tens of thousands of people. The isolation of rural life based on the single-family farm was replaced by a system where all social tasks were collectivized, from the harvest to education and health care. Communes across China even began to develop small-scale industry, which supplemented the large-scale capital-intensive industry still being developed. By the end of 1958, there were almost 25,000 communes.[6]

Despite high levels of mass mobilization and an initial increase in production, the Great Leap Forward faced a number of organiza-tional difficulties, many due to the still very low level of technology available for production. In the new communes, the problems of organizing social life within the framework of the first attempts at economic planning caused disruptions in production.

Compounding these problems, massive natural disasters struck in 1960, creating both a major humanitarian crisis and an economic setback. This took place at the same time that the Soviet Union withdrew all of its technicians and cancelled more than 600 technical aid and scientific contracts and projects, a development related to the Sino-Soviet split.[7]

These problems, combined with tense relations with the Soviet Union, led the Chinese government to change course in the early 1960s.

Borrowing from Soviet techniques being introduced under Khrushchev, the Chinese government expanded capitalist market methods and material incentives to increase production, and increased the authority of managers, technicians and planners. The social goals of increasing the weight of the working class and peasantry within the relations of production became secondary.

This had several effects. Increased power for managers and technicians strengthened bureaucratic elements in the government who saw themselves as separate from the working class, even though they were supposed to be working in the service of that class.

It also strengthened the political position of more conservative elements in the Communist Party, who used the difficulties during and following the Great Leap Forward as an opportunity to wage a political offensive against Mao Zedong and the other supporters of the "socialist road."

THE CULTURAL REVOLUTION

It was against this backdrop that the "two-line struggle"—an expression of contending class forces that existed in China following the victory of the revolution and that manifested themselves in the ideological and policy debate about the most efficient method for economic development—came to the forefront of Chinese politics. The left wing of the CPC was on the defensive at a critical time for the Chinese Revolution and the world struggle. The Communist Party of the Soviet Union was using its position in the communist movement to portray Mao and his allies as "ultra-lefts" as a way to justify their own conciliatory policy with U.S. imperialism.

Mao's main opponents within the Communist Party were Liu Shaoqi, a veteran member of the CPC who held the country's top governmental post, the chairman of the People's Republic of China, and Deng Xiaoping. They were the main proponents of reversing the course that Mao had initiated in the Great Leap Forward in favor of

Lin Biao: The goals of the Cultural Revolution

'Consolidate the dictatorship of the proletariat, develop socialism!'

On Oct. 1, 1966, 1.5 million Chinese students, Red Guards, workers and peasants filled Beijing's Tiananmen Square to celebrate the anniversary of China's revolution. Lin Biao, then Mao's closest ally and collaborator, addressed the crowd. He explained the significance of the Cultural Revolution that had officially been announced two months earlier.

TODAY, we are celebrating this great festival amidst the upsurge of the Great Proletarian Cultural Revolution. This revolution is a great revolution, an entirely new and creative revolution, carried out after the seizure of political power by the proletariat. It is to overthrow through struggle the small handful of persons within the Party who have been in authority and have taken the capitalist road, to sweep away all ghosts and monsters in our society, and to break the old ideas, culture, customs and habits of the proletariat, with a view to further consolidating the dictatorship of the proletariat and developing the socialist system. The historical experience of the dictatorship of the proletariat in the world teaches us that if we fail to do so, the rule of revisionism will come about and the restoration of capitalism will take place. Should this come to pass in our country, China would go back to its former colonial and semi-colonial, feudal and semi-feudal road, and the imperialist reactionaries would again ride roughshod over the people. The importance of our Great Proletarian Cultural Revolution is therefore perfectly clear.

market methods. Mao called Liu, Deng Xiaoping and their co-thinkers "capitalist roaders."

The re-introduction of market mechanisms in the countryside had sharpened the class struggle. As early as May 1963, Mao submitted a draft document to the CPC Central Committee called the

"First Ten Points." Biographer Han Suyin described the document: "It denounces the recrudescent [renewed] activity of landlords and rich peasants at this moment on the offensive in the countryside. ... Speculation and profiteering of serious proportions had occurred—buying and selling of land, usury, and extortion."[8]

Mao identified the growing struggle within the party as a manifestation of the class struggle. He warned that capitalism could gain the most in China by way of bourgeois ideas. Since the question of which class would rule was far from decisively settled, the class struggle would have to be carried into the realm of ideology.

The opening salvo of the Cultural Revolution came in the form of literary criticism. In November 1965, the Shanghai newspaper Wen Hui Pao published an article criticizing a play called "The Dismissal of Hai Jui."[9] The article accused the playwright of using the story of a Ming Dynasty official to criticize the party and Mao.

Since the author of the play was the deputy mayor of Beijing, it was clear that the criticism was not for the purpose of academic debate. The targets of the criticism were "capitalist roaders"—and they were found in the upper echelons of the CPC.

The Great Proletarian Cultural Revolution was officially announced in August 1966. The Central Committee of the CPC adopted the "Decision Concerning the Great Proletarian Cultural Revolution," also known as the "16 Points," which read in part:

> Although the bourgeoisie has been overthrown, it is still trying to use the old ideas, culture, customs and habits of the exploiting classes to corrupt the masses, capture their minds and endeavor to stage a comeback. The proletariat must do just the opposite: it must meet head-on every challenge of the bourgeoisie in the ideological field ... At present, our objective is to struggle against and overthrow those persons in authority who are taking the capitalist road, to criticize and repudiate the reactionary bourgeois academic 'authorities' and the ideology of the bourgeoisie ... and to transform education, literature and art and all other parts of the superstructure not in correspondance to the socialist economic base, so as to facilitate the consolidation and development of the socialist system.[10]

The impact of these and other articles initially stimulated a student movement in a few cities. First students, then teachers as well, began to put up wall posters by the thousands identifying particular school and government officials as "capitalist roaders." A series of statements and articles from Mao promoting the Cultural Revolution ignited a national movement. Millions of students across the country took part.

Not content to just put up posters, students began to openly denounce and replace school and government leaders. Although Mao and his allies in the Central Committee were the minority inside the leadership, their political ideas corresponded to the political thinking of millions of students and teachers, and increasingly growing layers of the working class.

U.S. and other western media normally glorify any protest or dissent within a country that has a socialist government. Championing the cause of workers and students against the "communist bureaucrats" is the norm. Even the smallest protest in Cuba or the former Soviet Union, or in China today, is promoted with great fanfare in the corporate media.

Not so in the Cultural Revolution. When millions of young people—later workers and peasants as well—participated in the Cultural Revolution against party leaders who were preserving privilege and inequality, the big business media treated them as dangerous lunatics.

The ruling class understood the meaning of this vast movement. This revolution was aimed at overcoming the problems of Chinese society by taking the next step in the direction of communism—rather than by returning to capitalism.

What was unique about Mao and Lin Biao's[11] campaign was that it appealed "over the heads" of the party leaders directly to the masses. This is in sharp contrast with the Leninist norms of democratic centralism that have been practiced by communist parties around the world. According to these norms, Mao would have restricted his criticisms to inner-party discussions during congresses and plenums. To the masses, the party would have maintained a united position. This was one of the criticisms cited by the revisionist Soviet leadership in calling the Cultural Revolution "ultra-left."

These criticisms ignored the fact that Lenin and the Bolsheviks adopted democratic centralism as the best way for a revolutionary political program to be put into practice. Appealing to formalism in order to justify a reactionary political program or practice has nothing in common with revolutionary Marxism.

Mao and his allies within the CPC concluded that they could not defeat the capitalist roaders without appealing to the masses. The form of the Cultural Revolution is secondary to its social content and objectives, which were to prevent the takeover of the Communist Party by those who desired to replace socialist methods with the return of capitalist property relations.

His appeal was simple: "Marxism consists of thousands of truths, but these truths can be summarized in the statement: It is right to rebel against reactionaries!"

ADVANCE AND RETREAT

Throughout 1967, more and more people were drawn into the Cultural Revolution. Old leaders were denounced and replaced by new leaders from the working class and from the youth. Mass meetings in government buildings and in the factories became routine. Revolutionary committees were created, becoming broad organizations of the masses of workers and peasants.

In January and February of 1967, workers in Shanghai launched what may have been the most advanced initiative of the entire Chinese Revolution. Revolutionary workers' organizations of Shanghai seized the city's two main newspapers and declared the "Shanghai Commune."[12] It was explicitly modeled on the example of the Paris Commune of March to May 1871, the first time that the working class seized and held political power. As in the Paris Commune, the Shanghai Commune had open elections of leaders, with the provision of automatic recall.

The direct intervention of the working class in the revolution was complicated and nuanced. New anarchist and communist factions developed within the workers' organizations. Meanwhile, the old guard who had been targeted as capitalist roaders was fighting back.

Concerned that they could not vanquish the influence of the capitalist roaders under these circumstances, Mao's leadership group retreated from the commune-style state as a model. Fearing that the growing struggles were leading to a large-scale violent confrontation, they chose to reassert the control of the bureaucracy to a certain extent. The result was a compromise.

Mao now promoted "three-in-one combination committees," sometimes called the Triple Alliance. Political power was exercised through committees with representatives of the mass youth, workers' and peasants' organizations, members of the People's Liberation Army and Communist Party cadres. By including this last category, Mao opened the door for party functionaries who had been ousted as capitalist roaders to regain a foothold in the state.

This was a retreat compared to the workers' and peasants' democracy that was emerging from the mass mobilization of the Cultural Revolution. It marked the beginning of the end of the Cultural Revolution. It marked a definite step away from the commune style of state that was beginning to emerge.

The Triple Alliance was a halfway measure that retained more democratic features compared to the government structures that had existed prior to the Cultural Revolution, but it also marked the re-entrenchment of the old establishment.

STABILIZATION

Every revolution includes a degree of chaos, arbitrary action and excess. This was certainly the case during the Cultural Revolution. But much of the reporting was distorted both by the world bourgeoisie, who feared the revolutionary mobilization, and by the Chinese leadership of the period who were the targets of the mass mobilizations.

Of course, this movement of millions, organized mainly through schools in "Red Guard" detachments, did cause a level of social upheaval. Every true revolution does.

But by 1968, the biggest mobilizations had subsided. The Triple Alliance was more or less in place in all parts of the country, with Mao's supporters occupying most of the high posts in the government.

With agricultural production increasing above the levels preceding the crisis that had begun in 1959, Chinese industry was able to continue to move forward. China had developed a method for producing a durable, low-alloy steel; they produced 30 times as much in 1969 than in 1965. By the early 1970s, self-sufficiency in cotton, wool and silk was achieved, and China was the world's largest producer of cotton. Production of tractors doubled in the first seven months of 1970 as compared to tractor production in all of 1966. China was producing more than 1,000 different models of agricultural machinery—300 more models than were produced in 1966.[13]

Communes remained the basic political and economic unit in the countryside, organized according to the Triple Alliance model. Each commune had its own schools, hospitals and medical centers. "Barefoot doctors" were trained in basic medical procedures, spreading access to basic health care to millions. In 1973, 50 percent of all medical students were women.

This was part of an overall heightening of the status of women in society. By 1971, 90 percent of women had jobs working outside of the home.[14]

THE SEEDS OF LATER STRUGGLES

Many historians mark the end of the Cultural Revolution with Mao's death in 1976 and the subsequent arrest of his closest allies. In fact, the Cultural Revolution as a mass outpouring of Chinese workers, peasants and students ended as early as 1969.

One of the factors that led to the end of this historic conflict was a bitter political struggle that broke out within the left wing of the CPC. The main advocates of the commune-style state, loosely grouped around Lin Biao and Chen Boda, came into conflict with Mao and the other left-wing section of the CPC. Many details of the conflict remain unknown in the world communist movement. But in 1971, Lin Biao died in a mysterious plane crash. That same year, Chen Boda dropped out of sight and would not be seen again until his arrest and imprisonment five years later.

In February 1972, U.S. president Richard Nixon visited China, a key chapter in the U.S.-China anti-Soviet rapprochement that had devastating political effects for China, the socialist camp and the world.

Between 1971 and Mao's death in 1976, the old capitalist roaders gradually reconciled their way back into positions of authority in the party. When Mao died, these forces had sufficient strength to oust the remaining leftists. Mao's closest allies during the period of the Cultural Revolution were publicly demonized, arrested and suppressed.

During the French Revolution that established the political rule of the bourgeoisie and uprooted the feudal ruling class, a period known as "The Terror" (1793-4) was necessary to remove the old ruling class from power. Tens of thousands of supporters of the old regime were executed. But The Terror was followed by a period of reaction known as the Thermidor, when the most conservative elements of the revolutionary coalition succeeded in driving out the Jacobin left wing and taking over.

The suppression of the left between 1976 and 1978 opened the Chinese Revolution's Thermidor. The impact of the sharp struggles for revolutionary socialism on the lives of millions of Chinese workers, peasants and students cannot be airbrushed away by revisionist history of Mao's political opponents, however. Even the Thermidor in France could not dislodge the aspirations of the working classes, who rose up again some 75 years later in the Paris Commune.

The chapters of class struggle in China remain a reserve source for the workers of China and the world in the struggle for revolutionary socialism. ☐

Endnotes

1. Arthur G. Ashbrook, Jr., *An Economic Profile of Mainland China* (New York, Praeger, 1968), 18, quoted in E.L. Wheelwright and Bruce McFarlane, *The Chinese Road to Socialism,* (New York, Monthly Review Press, 1970), 31.
2. E.L. Wheelwright and Bruce McFarlane, *The Chinese Road to Socialism,* 35-6, 39.
3. Han Suyin, *Wind in the Tower: Mao Tsetung and the Chinese Revolution 1949-1975,* (London, Jonathan Cape, 1976), 69.
4. Ibid, 124.
5. Historically, the "Great Leap Forward" is considered to be the 1958-1960 period, not the entirety of the five-year plan, because the CPC changed course prior to 1963.
6. E.L. Wheelwright and Bruce McFarlane, *The Chinese Road to Socialism,* 40.
7. "The Sino-Soviet Dispute," *Keesing's Research Report 3,* (New York, Charles Scribner's Sons, 1969), 29.
8. Han Suyin, *The Wind in the Tower,* 218.

9. The play was originally published in 1959.

10. "Decision Concerning the Great Proletarian Cultural Revolution," adopted on August 8, 1966, by the Central Committee of the CCP. Official English version published in R. Rojas, "La Guardia Roja Conquista China," 1968, 430-40.

11. Lin had been the leader of the People's Liberation Army and had been named Mao's constitutionally designated successor during the Cultural Revolution.

12. Mao Zedong, "Talk At A Meeting Of The Central Cultural Revolution Group," *Long Live Mao Tse-tung Thought,* a Red Guard Publication, January 9, 1967.

13. Maria Antonietta Macciocchi, *Daily Life in Revolutionary China,* (New York, Monthly Review Press, 1972), 208, 212, 214.

14. Ruth Sidel, *Women and Child Care in China,* (Baltimore, Penguin, 1973), 23-4.

APPENDIX

For the defense of China against counterrevolution, imperialist intervention and dismemberment

PARTY FOR SOCIALISM AND LIBERATION

The following document is the result of almost two years of deliberation and discussion by members of the Party for Socialism and Liberation. It was first distributed as part of pre-convention discussion for the party's 2006 convention. At that convention and then over the next year, it was the basis for party discussion and educational classes. It was adopted with amendments by the party's National Committee in May 2007.

The purpose of the document was twofold. First, its comprehensive scope and background material is designed to orient new activists to the PSL's understanding of the tremendously complex and fluid nature of the class struggle now taking place in China. Second, it is designed to prepare the party to politically intervene in the case of a sharpening of the class struggle in China and especially in the case of a U.S.-backed counterrevolution.

The document is reprinted here in the format that it was presented and discussed in the PSL, with points numbered for ease of discussion and reference.

THE CHINESE REVOLUTION: A HISTORIC ACHIEVEMENT

1) The Chinese Revolution of 1925 to 1949 was one of the greatest events and achievements in the history of the working-class struggle for emancipation. At the time of the victory of the Chinese socialist revolution over the imperialist-backed comprador capitalist state and Nationalist Party (Kuomintang), led by Chiang Kai-shek,

over 1 million people each year were dying from starvation. The Chinese people suffered from illiteracy, an epidemic of opium addiction, brutal oppression stemming from semi-feudal relations in the countryside, the severe all-sided oppression of women and the carving up of China into spheres of influence by the various European and Japanese imperialist powers.

2) Between 1949 and 1955, the Chinese people—with the leadership of the Communist Party of China—eradicated mass starvation, opium addiction and prostitution while making huge advances in wiping out illiteracy, providing health care for the people and stable employment for the urban working class, eliminating landlordism in the countryside, and many other social achievements that were almost unequaled in the history of humankind by their scope, reach and rapidity. By 1955, core industries had been nationalized and the beginnings of a planned economy began to take shape. The economic model was based on the overturning of capitalist property relations in the commanding heights of the economy.

3) China, under the leadership of the Communist Party in the 1950s, sought to reverse the century of humiliation at the hands of imperialism and colonialism, and quickly emerged as a beacon for colonized and semi-colonized peoples fighting for national liberation throughout Asia, Africa, Latin America and the Middle East.

THE SINO-SOVIET CONFLICT

4) Relations between Mao Zedong and the leadership of the Soviet Union—which had been formal, correct and comradely since the 1920s—included considerable tension as a consequence of the Soviet policy of official support for the pro-imperialist Nationalist Party led by Chiang Kai-shek. At the conclusion of World War II, for instance, the leadership of the Soviet Union formally recognized the Chiang Kai-shek government as the legitimate representative of the Chinese people, even though huge parts of China were then under the control of the Communist Party of China and its Red Army. In 1945, the Soviet leadership urged the Communist Party of China not to seek the overthrow of the Chiang government. While the nationwide civil war between the Communist Party and the Nationalist Party raged in the years leading up to the 1949 victory of the Communist Party,

the Soviet leadership maintained a Treaty of Friendship and Alliance (signed in 1945) with the Chiang government.

The retrograde and opportunist Soviet policy was based primarily on the fully understandable fear that imperialism would react to a socialist revolution in China by initiating a war against the Soviet Union. The United States had acquired nuclear weapons and used them just four years earlier. The Soviet leadership was primarily seeking a period of respite from war so that it could rebuild the country, which had lost more than 27 million people from the German Nazi invasion.

5) Immediately after the victory of the socialist revolution in China in 1949, Mao Zedong traveled to Moscow. After long negotiations, the two sides signed a Treaty of Friendship and Alliance in 1950 that paved the way for the creation of an economic, political and military united front between the Union of Soviet Socialist Republics and the People's Republic of China. The Soviet Union sent vast amounts of economic and military assistance, along with thousands of economic advisors and technicians, to help China's rapid economic ascent aimed at overcoming the legacy of colonial-imposed underdevelopment. The Soviet-Chinese alliance was the single greatest threat to imperialism and the single biggest hope to the entire world's people fighting to overcome colonialism and exploitation. At that time, more than two-fifths of the world's people lived in countries dedicated to socialist development.

6) A principal foreign policy objective of U.S. imperialism following the victory of the Chinese Revolution in 1949 was to break up the Soviet-Chinese alliance. The U.S. government learned from the experience with the Soviet-Yugoslavian split in 1948—and the consequent economic, political and even military embrace of Yugoslavia by western imperialism following that split—that another major cleavage inside the socialist bloc was possible. The endless threats against both China and the Soviet Union in the 1950s were accompanied by "feelers" from imperialism, raising the hope of rapprochement or accommodation with either the Soviet Union or China—at the expense of the other.

7) The consolidation of a new leadership in the Soviet Union in 1956 included the articulation of a new line by that leadership. The Khrushchev leadership promoted the line of "peaceful coexistence"

between imperialism and the socialist bloc countries. That line meant an incremental policy of rapprochement or détente with imperialism.

"Summit diplomacy" between the Soviet and U.S. leaders began in the late 1950s with high-level and super-high-visibility meetings between Khrushchev and western imperialist leaders. At the same time, closed-door bilateral negotiations on nuclear weapons testing and other issues were taking place. In 1963, the United States and the Soviet Union signed the Nuclear Test Ban Treaty banning the atmospheric testing of atomic and hydrogen bombs. While the diminution of war tensions between the Soviet Union and the United States was positive for socialist construction in the Soviet Union, and the ban on atmospheric tests of nuclear bombs was a big step forward in eliminating the lingering nuclear fallout from such tests, the bilateral negotiations had a harmful effect on Soviet-Chinese relations. The closed talks contributed to China's feeling of isolation precisely during the years that Washington was engaged in stepped up threats against China. China had been denied entrance into the United Nations. Additionally, the Pentagon was arming Chiang Kai-shek's regime to the teeth as it engaged in an ongoing missile and bombing war against the People's Republic of China from its perch in Taiwan.

8) China's leadership initiated a political polemic in the late 1950s against the Soviet leadership for its political line of accommodation with imperialism at the expense of China and those fighting for national liberation against the same imperialist countries.

9) The Sino-Soviet political ideological struggle corresponded initially to a sharp leftward swing by the Chinese leadership. The Communist Party of China helped revive on an international scale a critique of opportunism within the socialist movement similar to Lenin's original polemic against the leadership of the Second International in 1914. China's swing to the left in the 1960s contributed mightily to the global radicalization of that decade. China sought to overcome the isolation caused by the U.S.-Soviet relationship by promoting world revolution on all continents.

INDONESIAN COUNTERREVOLUTION
CONTRIBUTED TO CHINA'S ISOLATION

10) The U.S.-backed overthrow of the revolutionary nationalist Indonesian government in 1965, accompanied by the slaughter of

nearly 2 million Indonesians and the liquidation of the Indonesian Communist Party (the largest communist party outside of the socialist countries), deprived China of its principal ally. Indonesia, one of the most populous countries in the world, fell under a fascistic military dictatorship. Rather than being an ally of the Chinese Revolution, Indonesia turned into its opposite. The effect on China's leadership cannot be overestimated. By way of historical analogy, the impact on China of the defeat in Indonesia in 1965 was comparable to the impact on the newborn Soviet state of the defeat of the German revolution in 1923. Both of these setbacks were located on the international stage and outside the frontiers of the struggling socialist governments, but both contributed to the eventual consolidation of a conservative, non-revolutionary international foreign policy, which took shape in the Soviet Union in 1924 and in China by 1971.

11) As China became more isolated, its polemic with the Soviet leadership deteriorated badly starting in 1967 and 1968 with their characterization of the Soviet Union as a "social-imperialist" and even a "fascist" country. The Communist Party of China asserted that capitalism had been restored in the Soviet Union and thus declared that the Soviet Union was no different than the imperialist countries. No real evidence was offered for such a radical conclusion—nor could there have been, since the characterization of the Soviet Union as a capitalist social entity was without fact. It was not based on a scientific examination of Soviet society. This proved itself to be a fatal flaw in China's political and diplomatic orientation, and opened the gates for its own eventual rapprochement with U.S. imperialism as an ally against the Soviet Union. The ideological and political struggle devolved into a struggle between socialist states.

Both China and the Soviet Union were socialist countries in the popularly accepted but imprecise definition of the term. Both had a mode of production based on public rather private ownership. Both had centralized economic planning as the driving engine of the economy, rather than the drive for profit that characterizes capitalist economies. Both countries employed a strict monopoly of foreign trade, excluding imperialist intervention in the economy except when permitted and regulated by the government, thus severing the umbilical chord between imperialism and the enterprises on their own soil. Both China and the Soviet Union provided military and economic aid to the heroic people of Vietnam in their long war to evict the imperialist invaders. Both provided limited but essential assistance to other socialist countries and national liberation movements.

The U.S. opening to China in 1971 and 1972, following secret negotiations between Henry Kissinger, Richard Nixon and the Chinese leadership, led to the surprise resumption of U.S.-China diplomatic relations. From a Leninist view, such diplomatic relations, or what are called normalized relations, are entirely appropriate and even necessary from the vantage point of promoting socialist construction. The socialist countries need peace more than all else so that precious resources can be used to meet people's needs rather than for weapons. But China's normalization of relations with U.S. imperialism went a step further, since they were in essence premised on an anti-Soviet alliance. China's false characterization of the Soviet Union as an enemy state rather than a politically wayward socialist ally provided the political cover for the Chinese leadership to seal its own fully opportunist orientation toward imperialism.

This marked the end of the heroic era of China's revolutionary foreign policy. China's revolutionary internationalism in the 1960s had not contributed to its escape from isolation in relation to other states, but it had made China's prestige with the oppressed people of the world second to none. As economically poor and underdeveloped as China still was in the 1960s, it enjoyed the moral authority that comes with being the champion of the oppressed people against the exploiters and oppressors of the world.

THE NORMALIZATION OF DIPLOMATIC RELATIONS WITH THE UNITED STATES AND THE SPLIT WITHIN THE LEFT WING OF THE CPC

12) China's normalization of relations with U.S. imperialism on the basis of a consummation of an alliance against a sister socialist country signaled the transformation of China's internationalism into a dangerous expression of narrow nationalism and betrayal of class loyalty. It was an expression of classic opportunism, meaning that it put perceived short-term organizational gains ahead of the long-term interests of the world's working class. As such, it severely weakened Mao and the left wing of the Communist Party of China.

13) Between 1969 and 1971, the left wing of the Communist Party of China grouped around Mao Zedong and Lin Biao split into a bloody struggle. Lin had been the leader of the People's Liberation Army and had been named Mao's constitutionally designated successor during the Cultural Revolution. The struggle between them ultimately ended with Lin's death in a suspicious plane crash in 1971. The probable issue provoking the split—much remains hidden to this day—was Mao's decision to seek an accommodation with U.S. imperialism. Prior to Kissinger's surprise trip to Beijing in 1971, subsequent trips by him and Nixon later in 1971 and 1972, and the restoration of U.S.-China relations, there was a massive purge in the army and party of the supporters of Lin Biao and the left wing. The facts of the purge within the left were hidden from the masses of people and shrouded in all sorts of scurrilous and fantastic explanations. This has contributed in part to an insufficient examination and analysis of the importance that this intra-left struggle played in the eventual triumph of the more conservative leadership immediately following the death of Mao in 1976.

14) The almost instantaneous arrest and purge of the rest of the Maoist left wing following Mao's death in 1976 marked the complete end of the left-wing chapter of the Chinese Revolution. Those in the Communist Party leadership who had been characterized as "capitalist roaders" during the internal struggles of the 1960s now took the reins of power. Within a few years, these forces began on a path of a historic reorientation of the socialist economy. Starting in 1978, this marked the beginning of so-called "socialist market economy" in China.

TWO-LINE STRUGGLE:
WHICH PATH TO OVERCOME UNDERDEVELOPMENT?

15) Since its victory in 1949, the leadership of the Communist Party has by necessity been focused on the question of China's economic development. Staggering underdevelopment and poverty, with all of their attendant social problems, were the dominant legacy left by the old semi-feudal and bureaucratic capitalist social order. Affecting the day-to-day lives of more than 1 billion people, no task was more urgent than economic and social development. On this all wings of the Communist Party agreed.

But a protracted "two-line struggle" emerged within the party between Mao Zedong and his chief political rivals, Deng Xiaoping and Liu Shaoqi. The Mao grouping advocated socialist methods for development, including nationalized public property in the core industries and banking, centralized planning, collectivized agriculture, and a monopoly of foreign trade. The faction led by Liu and Deng was essentially pragmatic rather than Marxist in their approach. Characterized as "capitalist roaders" by the Mao faction during the activist phase of the Cultural Revolution of 1966 to 1969, the Deng faction took power in 1978. They began instituting a series of far-reaching economic reforms that became known as "market socialism" or "socialism with Chinese characteristics."

These reforms also led to the "opening up" of China to imperialist banks and corporations. The development strategy behind the "opening up" was premised on a strategic assumption: the lure of super profits from the employment of low-wage labor in China would lead to massive capital investment by the industries and banks that possessed the most advanced technology. China would benefit in its development by accessing and acquiring the latest technologies.

The Chinese commune system of collectivized agriculture was also dismantled and the Chinese countryside, known throughout Asia in the decades prior to 1970 for its egalitarian achievements and social gains for the poorest peasants, became severely stratified again.

While millions of more well-to-do peasants saw a sharp rise in their living standards, a huge mass of rural dwellers lost everything. Left to fend for themselves, they migrated by the tens of millions to urban areas seeking employment in newly created factories—many in special economic zones set aside for outside capitalist investors. This migrant labor force, uprooted from the land, became the source of human material necessary for the establishment of a new market-based private capitalist sector.

16) It is false to portray the two-line struggle—between the "capitalist roaders" led by Liu, Deng and their political heirs on one side, and the Mao grouping favoring socialist methods on the other—as a fight between those who favored rapid economic development using the import of foreign capital and the formation of an internal capitalist market as a stimulant on the one hand, and those who insisted on a slower tempo but with the preservation of socialist

norms on the other. Both sides in the two-line struggle put the rapid economic development of China as a top priority.

17) The Deng grouping argued initially that the material prerequisites for constructing socialism required a rapid acceleration of the building of China's productive forces, and that the import of foreign (imperialist) capital and technology was the fastest way to build up the productive forces.

During the Mao era, the Chinese economy was far from being a basket case. In fact, between 1952 and Mao's death in 1976, industrial output increased at an annual rate of 11.2 percent. Even including the most intensive upheavals and disruptions to production caused by the civil strife associated with the Cultural Revolution, industrial production grew at an annual average rate of 10 percent.[1] China did this with almost no foreign aid or assistance. All Soviet economic aid, assistance and advisors had been withdrawn by 1961, and China received few international bank loans. In fact, China was one of the very few Third World countries that entered the decade of the 1980s with almost no foreign debt hanging over its head.[2]

While China's tenfold increase in industrial production during the Mao era was a breathtaking advance, the progress in the impoverished rural villages and countryside was significantly slower. Overall agricultural production increased twofold during the same period. Although the annual living standards among the rural population only increased by about 1 percent during the 1952-76 period,[3] Chinese peasants enjoyed huge advances in public health, free public education, affordable housing and social security as a result of collectivization and the commune system. The extreme cleavage between rich and poor in the countryside was reduced. Although the growth in agriculture lacked the tempestuous growth of the industrial sector, it is noteworthy that "China grew 30-40 percent more food than India on 14 percent less arable land than India"during the same time period.[4]

THE TWO-LINE STRUGGLE REFLECTED
THE CLASS STRUGGLE DURING THE DICTATORSHIP
OF THE PROLETARIAT

18) The two-line struggle inside the Communist Party of China over which path of development to take in overcoming China's extreme underdevelopment was not merely an ideological and policy

debate about the most efficient method for economic development. It was an expression of contending class forces that existed in China following the victory of the revolution in 1949. The destruction of the Chiang Kai-shek army and its subsequent retreat to the island of Taiwan constituted a historic event. It was the smashing of the old state apparatus and its replacement by a new state force—the Red Army led by the Communist Party—that created the basis and the foundation of the new society. It replaced the dictatorship of the semi-feudal and comprador bourgeois state with a workers' state, or what is called in Marxist terminology the dictatorship of the proletariat.

But the replacement of the old state based on the class rule of the capitalists and big landowners with a new state based on the power of the working class does not in any way eliminate the class divide in society. Nor does the expropriation of the core means of production and the nationalization of capitalist private property settle the question of socialism. On the contrary, the expropriation of the big bourgeoisie and semi-feudal landowning class only raises the possibility of socialism. It creates the basis for the start of a transition to the lowest stage of communism, which Marx called socialism.

19) The line pursued by Mao and his faction(s) inside the Communist Party was premised on the need for the social and economic system to serve the needs of the working class and peasantry, first and foremost. The revolutionary process itself, including 22 consecutive years of armed struggle, imperialist invasion and civil war, culminated in the victory of the Communist Party because it relied on the organization, self-sacrifice and energy of the poor, the oppressed and the downtrodden. The revolutionary war itself aroused the masses of the peasants from their atomized and politically frozen status and, under the leadership of a working-class organization, transformed them into the activated social base for the new society.

20) The expropriation of the big capitalists between 1952 and 1955, the establishment of socialist planning for economic production and distribution, and the establishment of a state-based monopoly of foreign trade served a twofold function: first, to reclaim China's economic and political sovereignty and independence (in Mao's first speech in 1949 at Tiananmen Square he announced that the victory of the revolution meant that the Chinese people had "stood up"); and second, to place the society and its productive powers at the disposal

of the workers and peasants of China, who had emerged as the new ruling class, to meet their individual and social needs.

WORKING CLASS CANNOT BE THE LINK
TO WORLD CAPITALISM

21) In contrast to the Mao line, the "capitalist roaders" believed that the quickest road to development was the integration of China into the world capitalist market, with China carving out for itself a place in world capitalism's global division of labor as a low-wage, low-cost manufacturer of exports for a world market. They asserted that China's contribution to the international division of labor was not merely to provide a huge pool of labor available to work at low wages (low according to the standards prevailing for the working class in advanced capitalist countries), but also to offer a unique emerging market for the sale of commodities and especially for the export of surplus capital (factories, banks and finance capital, and so forth) from transnational capitalist corporations in the United States, Western Europe, Japan and elsewhere. The most unique feature of this emerging market was its size. Based on its population and economic development, China clearly offers capitalist investors a potential market, over time, equal in magnitude to the development of Western Europe and the United States a century ago.

22) The working class and the poor and middle peasants are not equipped as a class to be the link to world capitalism with its needs for super-exploitation, deal making and financial investment on a large scale in China. In fact, the working class and peasantry have interests that are antagonistic to the needs of capital. The country of origin for investment capital is completely immaterial to the proletariat. Capital, above all else, is a social relationship between exploiters and exploited. Capital thrives only through exploitation; that is, through the private appropriation and accumulation of surplus value created by collective, living labor. Whether Chinese workers are employed by capitalists from the United States, Germany or Japan, or whether the factory owner is a Chinese capitalist, the relationship is based on exploitation. It is a form of slavery for the wage-earning class.

23) Moreover, the class instinct of the Chinese proletariat would be to resist the demands of globalized international capital and its agents inside of China, who pursue a path of relentless cost-cutting

to remain competitive whether they are in the world capitalist market, in the Asia-wide regional market or in the emerging internal Chinese market. Cutting wages and social benefits, uprooting working-class neighborhoods for commercial development, and grabbing land in the countryside for capitalist development are typical features of the march of capital. The working class as a class is compelled to resist these incursions, and the phenomenon of class resistance is becoming widespread throughout China.

24) The economic reforms instituted since 1978 have eviscerated many of the social insurance guarantees previously enjoyed by the workers and more numerous peasantry. Basic social rights—health-care coverage for all, the right to a job, free public education and affordable housing—have been severely cut back for millions.

THE NEW CHINESE CAPITALIST CLASS
IS NOT HOMOGENEOUS

25) The reforms have spawned a new Chinese capitalist class. It is this capitalist class that is able to connect as partners with the transnational banks and corporations.

26) The Chinese capitalist class, like all class formations, is not homogenous. It is, after all, a class based on competition. It competes within itself for "market share" and for a place in the world economy. Its relationship with imperialist banks and corporations is not seamless and without conflict. World imperialism seeks to dominate the Chinese market for its own advantage.

27) There is undoubtedly a nationalist sector of the Chinese bourgeoisie that is in conflict with imperialism because it seeks to be the master over the Chinese economy and the internal market. Like many bourgeoisies in the colonial world, it resents the intrusion of imperialism because it desires to be the exploiter of its home markets rather than being run roughshod over by foreign imperialism. This phenomenon is universal within the formerly colonized and semi-colonized world. By way of one example, it is important to remember that the Cuban July 26 Movement included large sectors of the Cuban nationalist bourgeoisie who fought against the comprador Batista dictatorship, but then deserted the revolution and became accomplices of imperialism as it became evident that the Cuban working class was intent on holding the reins of power following the toppling of Batista in 1959.

28) Also there must be considerable segments within the rapidly emerging Chinese capitalist class, the urban middle class and the bourgeois intelligentsia who recognize that China's development requires a strong state to negotiate the terms of development within the boundaries of the existing world capitalist system. The Chinese bourgeoisie was too weak as a class to function as anything other than a proxy—a comprador or a puppet—of foreign capitalist interests prior to the 1949 revolution and the creation of a dictatorship of the proletariat. The development of western and Japanese capitalism into imperialism in the latter years of the 19th century had the effect of choking off the ability of the capitalists in the colonized and semi-colonized countries to follow the same path of development as a modern-day, mature ruling class. Throughout Asia, Africa, the Middle East and Latin America, the bourgeoisie's development as a class was stifled or retarded by the incursions of the foreign imperialist bourgeoisie. This process is documented and analyzed from a Marxist point of view in Walter Rodney's groundbreaking work "How Europe Underdeveloped Africa."

THE MONOPOLY OF FOREIGN TRADE

29) When the Communist Party of China came to power, it instituted the state's monopoly of foreign trade, severing the link between the Chinese bourgeoisie and world imperialism. It erected a new wall of China, one that was a thousand more times effective than the literal Great Wall of China in preventing the foreigners (today, the imperialists) from penetrating the country. Through the lever of the state and, moreover, the proletarian state dictatorship, China was able to retake control of its vast territory, natural resources and labor to begin on the path of real development in all economic, social and political spheres. The monopoly was an essential first step in preventing the looting and destruction of the country by those who had no interest in China or its people, and who saw both the natural and social landscape of east and central Asia as nothing more than a zone for pillage and "legalized" looting for their own profit.

30) The monopoly of foreign trade was fundamental for China's achievement of economic sovereignty. It functioned as a protective wall preventing spontaneous or unregulated contact between imperialism and domestic enterprises. The monopoly of foreign trade is

not a principal of socialism, but rather a method of protecting the domestic socialist economy from the ravaging effects of global capitalism, in particular from the transnational corporations and finance or bank capital. It is an expression of strength by the workers' state. But in some ways, even more, it is a measure of weakness by a single national economy trying to use socialist methods in the face of a world economy still dominated by capital. The monopoly of foreign trade is, like all things, a unity of opposites and contains within itself its own essential contradictions. The downside of the monopoly of foreign trade is that the wall that the socialist state erects to protect its economy from world capital can serve as an obstacle in accessing the latest advances in industrial and scientific technique. Access to technology is of utmost importance in the advancement and improvement of the productive forces. Any and all leadership, in both the economic and political arena, is keenly aware of the centrality of this issue. In the final analysis and over time, improvement in technique is the key to economic progress, and the idea of falling behind causes great fear because those who do so lose their political and economic legitimacy.

31) In the contest between the so-called great imperialist powers and China, the issue of falling behind in the development or improvement of industrial and scientific technique has fearful military consequences as well. It is clear from the history of the Soviet Union that it was the fear of imperialist war and aggression that compelled the government to constantly divert and refocus precious industrial, scientific and engineering resources to keep up with U.S. imperialism's "arms race."

32) The cruel paradox for a country such as China is that in order to speed up its economic and technological development, it has sought to engage or integrate into the world economy. But the world economy today is a world capitalist economy. The price for admission into this club is that China play by the rules of the world capitalist economy. This means access on the part of the imperialists to labor and markets; the penetration of finance capital not only as creditor, but also as director of industrial resources; and the right to a flexible pool of "free labor."

33) While world imperialism enjoys a virtual monopoly on technology and credit, without which international investment and trade

stagnate, all of its significant corporate components insist that China end or loosen the monopoly of foreign trade—the very foundation of a system that allowed China to regain its sovereignty and remedy its status of neo-colonial bondage.

34) With each new step in the reform process, as China becomes increasingly integrated into the world economy, the role of the Chinese state as the arbiter between Chinese enterprises and the transnational banks and corporations becomes further weakened and compromised. The Chinese capitalist class and the Communist Party are both supremely aware of this contradiction. A strong state that is focused on China's national interests, as opposed to a comprador-based state, is essential both to the independence and economic development of China's working class and peasantry, and to the development of the indigenous Chinese capitalists. If the imperialists have entirely unfettered access to China's markets and resources, the interests of both the working class and the emerging Chinese bourgeoisie will be trampled, reducing the latter to a secondary comprador layer.

IMPERIALISM'S ATTITUDE TOWARD THE CHINESE STATE

35) There is no indication that the destruction of the existing Chinese government, or the overthrow of the Communist Party of China under the current circumstances, could open the road to a more revolutionary government, the return of the primary use of socialist methods, or the expropriation of the international bourgeoisie that is "doing business" in China. On the contrary, the suspension of the current state would plunge China into the neo-colonial abyss. Caring not one iota for China's development as a nation, much less the interests of the working class or peasants, each foreign imperialist corporation or bank would scorch the country in an unfettered search for super profits. The likely outcome of this scenario would be that China would not only be thrown back from its dynamic forward march, but the country could easily splinter—the imperialists would take control of the "valuable" coastal areas, while the other areas would wither away.

36) We have seen from what has happened with the imperialist destruction of the bourgeois nationalist regime in Iraq the kind of centrifugal dangers that loom. China has a long history with this process; all classes are keenly aware that it was the basis for China's "century

of humiliation," whereby the country was divided up by the combination of foreign spheres of influence and regionally based warlordism.

THE 'RULE OF LAW'

37) The imperialists want to weaken the influence of the Chinese state, which has been led by the Communist Party of China since 1949. The imperialists demand that the state intervention in the economy be replaced by the so-called "rule of law." By "law," however, the U.S. government and U.S.-based capitalist entities mean nothing other than the "rules and regulations" for capitalist investment, deal making and property rights for transnational corporations. The much-vaunted "rule of law" championed by U.S. imperialism is a high-sounding euphemism for the replacement of any vestige of the monopoly of foreign trade with "laws" that put the rights of property—specifically U.S. property and exported capital—ahead of the rights of China's workers.

38) The ever-present demand that China adopt the "rule of law" is largely a one-way street. When the Chinese state-owned company CNOOC attempted to purchase a third-tier U.S.-based oil company, UNOCAL, in 2005, offering a higher bid than any other capitalist competitor, the U.S. government went into a nearly full mobilization, threatening China and demanding that China forget about acquiring a "strategic" U.S.-owned asset. Congress demanded immediate action to stop the acquisition. The Washington Post reported, "Now, China has added national security concerns to economic anxieties, with lawmakers expressing fear that China is aggressively seeking to corner a strategic asset, oil, and create its own captive supply. ... House and Senate members demanded an administration review of the bid, required under the Defense Production Act, to determine potential economic and security risks. Treasury officials indicated they would agree to the request if UNOCAL accepts CNOOC's offer." UNOCAL turned down the Chinese company's offer, accepting a lower bid from another takeover corporation. Meanwhile, U.S. banks and corporations are aggressively moving to buy entirely or to become full partners in China's banking, telecommunications, energy and other "strategic" economic sectors. The "rule of law"—or the rule of the "free" market—apparently only applies when it is beneficial to U.S. corporate interests.

IMPERIALISM SEEKS TO MANIPULATE
WORKERS' GRIEVANCES

39) The U.S. government, the media, right-wing organizations, a coalition of liberal and conservative politicians in Congress, and key sectors of the U.S. labor bureaucracy agitate regularly against the Chinese government. There is a constant effort to delegitimize the Chinese state at the same time as they are doing business with and through the state. The imperialist powers, whose economic intervention and penetration has caused so much class polarization inside of China, even demagogically champion the cause of the Chinese workers and peasants when they rebel against the government for implementing policies that the same imperialists insist on as a condition for "doing business."

This is precisely what the Reagan administration and the CIA, with the help of the anti-communist AFL-CIO leadership, did with their support in 1981 for the Polish workers when they were mobilized under the leadership of Solidarity, a CIA-backed "independent" Polish union, against the Polish government. The Polish government, led by the ruling communist United Workers Party, had decollectivized agriculture and integrated the national economy into the world capitalist economy as an exporter. When the working class suffered economically as a result of the Polish government agreeing to policies demanded by U.S. banks as a condition for a further extension of credit, the same banks, the CIA and the whole imperialist establishment became the champion of the workers movement against the socialist government. The delegitimizing of the United Workers Party in the early 1980s was really the first step in a decade of counterrevolution that eventually led to the overthrow of the Polish government, all of the socialist-bloc governments of Eastern Europe and finally of the Soviet Union.

40) In China today, there are a growing number of spontaneous struggles by workers and rural dwellers against capitalist abuses over a whole range of issues. There have been reports of widespread protests against regional and national government decisions that have favored commercial interests over the workers, peasants and local communities. In some of these cases, the government has apparently resorted to police methods of violence and repression to restore public order. Frequently, police repression has fueled greater resistance and

resentment from the people. The use of violence against these protests has the danger of alienating the Communist Party of China from its social base among the oppressed classes.

In these spontaneous protests, communists everywhere stand with the working class and peasantry as they advance their own class interests. Of course, in evaluating our position in regard to any struggle, we must keep our eyes wide open to the danger that the leadership of legitimate struggles of the workers and peasants could be taken over by counterrevolutionary and pro-imperialist elements— especially when the working class lacks revolutionary leadership. That is an entirely different matter.

CHINA'S FOREIGN POLICY:
NATIONALISM VERSUS INTERNATIONALISM

41) China's relationship with the United States is only one element of its global orientation expressed through its foreign policy. But its relationship with and policy toward U.S. imperialism is decisive, defining all other aspects of its international orientation. China is following a nationalist rather than a proletarian internationalist political line and program. This is not a pejorative description or characterization of the line of the CPC. It is their stated policy. China's stated goal is to transform from "an underdeveloped country to a medium level developed country" by the middle of the 21st century.[5]

The CPC considers that for this to happen it must maintain "good relations" with the United States, which it understands can only happen by recognizing U.S. imperialism's global interests, especially its most vital ones. This explains why China has gone out of its way to avoid confrontation with the United States in the Middle East, an area considered by the United States to be of pre-eminent strategic significance because of its oil and natural gas reserves. Although China had important relations with Iraq, Iran and other targets of U.S. imperialism, it is trying to do everything it can to minimize confrontation with U.S. imperialism. Its policy is based on appeasing the beast so as to avoid having the beast's wrath shifted toward China. In the 1990s, China supported economic sanctions on Iraq and refused to use its role in the Security Council to condemn the U.S. war against Iraq. On Feb. 4, 2006, China voted with the United States to refer Iran to the U.N. Security Council on the issue of Iran's nuclear development.

At first glance, these moves appear to harm China's national interests. Even putting aside the communist internationalist obligation to stand with oppressed nations against imperialism, these moves appear to sacrifice China's narrow national interests insofar as they harm its key allies and strengthen the hand of an imperialist power that is clearly still antagonistic to China. But China's foreign policy, with its own economic development as the number one priority, is built upon two interconnected goals: first, to avoid an open conflict with U.S. imperialism at a time when it has entered its most aggressive and lethal stage; and second, to have China engaged in rather than isolated from the forces of economic globalization.[6]

One of the top advisors to Chinese President Hu Jintao described this orientation recently in a way that would be perfectly understandable to the entire imperialist establishment: "China's peaceful rise is focused on ensuring the rights of subsistence, development and education to the 1.3 to 1.5 billion Chinese people and [thus] ensuring one fourth of the world's population a decent and dignified life. **This is fundamentally different from the era of Brezhnev, when the Soviet Communist Party, under the slogan of 'world revolution,' tried to seek hegemony through military expansion.**"[7] [emphasis added] Of course, this statement is loaded with irony given the fact that it was Brezhnev who accused Mao and the Chinese of promoting "world revolution." Irony aside, this is a clear message from the Chinese leadership to imperialism about its intentions and its orientation.

42) The Chinese government and the Communist Party have developed a nationalist-focused foreign policy over a three-decade period. In the 1960s, when it pursued a foreign policy based on revolutionary internationalism, China's prestige among the people of the world was at its zenith. Tens of millions of people on all continents identified with China or with Maoism, including in the United States. Mao's issuing the "Letter to the Afro-American people" in 1962 and providing refuge in Beijing to civil rights activist Robert Williams, who was being persecuted by the FBI, were just two of many examples where China's support for oppressed peoples and its defiance of imperialism made it a beacon of hope and inspiration. On all continents, it strengthened the hand of communist ideology among those forces fighting for national liberation.

CHINA EXCLUDED FROM THE IMPERIALIST CLUB

43) Although China's foreign policy is based first and foremost on accommodation with imperialism, it is well recognized within the summits of the CPC that China is not a member of the imperialist club. Moreover, the CPC recognizes that "in terms of state-to-state affairs, China and the United States cannot hope to establish truly friendly relations"[8] as exist among the imperialist nations. China is fixing its policy in accordance with the view that "at least for the next several years, Washington will not regard Beijing as its main security threat, and China will avoid antagonizing the United States."[9] This is according to Wang Jisi, director of the Institute of Strategic Studies at the Central Party School of the Communist Party of China.

44) There are vast differences between the current U.S.-China relationship and the post-World War II U.S.-Soviet relationship, which is popularly known under the false and misleading label of the "Cold War." The Soviet Union was the anchor for a global camp of socialist governments. Its fundamental relationship was based on razor-sharp confrontation. The two global class camps competed with each other on all fronts: military, economic, diplomatic and ideological. The ever-present danger of war, including global thermonuclear war, was right at the surface of international politics. China's collaboration with or appeasement of U.S. foreign policy objectives, on the other hand, coupled with its engagement in the global capitalist economy, including large-scale U.S. corporate and banking investment in and partnership with China, has had the effect of mitigating the underlying tension and hostility. But the tension and hostility has not vanished—nor can it.

45) While the political line of the Communist Party of China has had the effect of creating illusions about imperialism's intentions in China and allowed for the growth of imperialism's class allies in China, the official foreign policy of China is premised on the recognition that the U.S.-China relationship is inherently unstable. The U.S. government rests on the foundation of imperialist global interests while the Chinese government's foundational base is a socialist revolution in an underdeveloped country. The fact that the Chinese government has introduced capitalist economic relations in increasingly large sectors of the economy has not erased this fundamental

antagonism in spite of many areas of cooperation and, on China's part, appeasement and accommodation with imperialism.

Wang Jisi's article, unofficially representing the Communist Party's position on U.S.-China relations, dispassionately explained the nature of the underlying relationship. The article uses bourgeois rather than Marxist terminology. It is noteworthy, however, for its underlying analysis, which provides the framework for China's strategic orientation toward U.S. imperialism: "The Chinese-U.S. relationship remains beset by more differences than any other bilateral relationship between major powers in the world today. It is an extremely complex and highly paradoxical unity of opposites. It is not a relationship of confrontation and rivalry for primacy, as the U.S.-Soviet relationship was during the Cold War, but it does feed some of the same characteristics. ... The tremendous gap between the two countries in national and international power and the international status and the fundamental differences between their political systems and ideology have prevented the United States from viewing China as a peer. ... It is thus only natural that in their exchanges, the United States should take the offensive role and China the defensive one."[10]

Note the characterization of the U.S.-Soviet relationship as a "rivalry for [global] primacy." This mischaracterizes the objectives of the Soviet Union in that global class confrontation, though it does include a very big kernel of truth. The writer distinguishes the difference between today's U.S.-China relationship with that of the prior U.S.-Soviet "rivalry" based on seeking "primacy," but he does not suggest that the United States is not still seeking global primacy. On the contrary, this truth is assumed and taken for granted.

The Soviet Union was not an imperialist power. It assumed the leadership of a global force that checked, and at times confronted, U.S. imperialism in its pursuit of empire and global domination. The article assures bourgeois public opinion and U.S. policymakers that China has no such intention of confronting U.S. hegemonic ambitions—unless, that is, those ambitions directly menace China. But the article implicitly recognizes that even with the desire to appease U.S. ambitions, China cannot escape the offensive advances of U.S. imperialism. Instead, China seeks to manage the complex relationship by mitigating the imperialist offensive, particularly as it concerns U.S. and Japanese machinations and plans in Asia.

THE CLASS CHARACTER OF THE CHINESE REVOLUTION

46) The 1949 Chinese Revolution was a socialist revolution in the sense that it was based on the triumph of a new power: the working class and peasantry. Despite the Communist Party of China's initial description of the new government as a "bloc of four classes"—the working class, the peasantry, the urban petty bourgeoisie and the national bourgeoisie—the new state structure was in essence the dictatorship of the proletariat.

47) The Chinese Revolution was correctly described by Sam Marcy in 1950 as the dictatorship of the proletariat, although not in the "chemically pure" sense, because its essential feature included the destruction of the old state power—the comprador capitalist army of Chiang Kai-shek—and its replacement by the Red Army. The communist-led Red Army had existed as a guerrilla army for two decades. Its social foundation was primarily the peasantry, with smaller representation of the working class. However, the fact that the Red Army was largely composed of peasants rather than the urban proletariat did not make it fundamentally a peasant army. The officer corps of the Red Army was made up of cadre from the Communist Party of China, a party based on a proletarian world outlook and a communist program that corresponded to the needs and aspirations of the socially collectivized Chinese proletariat.

48) The characterization of the Chinese Revolution as a "workers' state," or, to use more technically precise Marxist language, the dictatorship of the proletariat, was completely validated by the actual experience of China's evolution within a few years following the 1949 victory. The new state took slow steps against capital between 1949 and 1952. The commanding heights of the capitalist industrial economy and the banking system were essentially nationalized by 1955. The establishment of the commune system in the countryside reorganized agriculture on a collectivized basis. China's social course was further evidenced in the realm of international relations. Despite severe tensions between the Chinese communist leadership and the leadership of the Soviet Union, a bond of practical unity was established, including bilateral economic ties that were socialist rather than exploitative at their core.

49) During the 1950s, the orientation of the Communist Party of China and the new dictatorship of the proletariat toward the indigenous bourgeoisie and national capitalists—meaning those who had not embraced Chiang Kai-shek or his U.S. imperialist masters—was largely benevolent. Despite the fact that many bourgeois forces lost legal possession of their property, and despite the fact that the privileges enjoyed by the petty bourgeoisie and bourgeois intelligentsia were relatively restricted compared to "Old China," many of these forces were incorporated into the new or "socialist" China. They were considered useful and necessary as managers, technicians, specialists and educators in a country that was thoroughly ravaged by illiteracy, poverty and underdevelopment. They received significant privileges, relative to the workers and peasants, in exchange for their services. Although they were not capitalist owners in the proper sense, they remained nonetheless a privileged sector. Their preponderant social and political weight was felt not only inside the state apparatus and the economy.

THE BOURGEOISIE AND THE WORKERS' STATE

50) As the bourgeoisie learned to do while it was an oppressed class in feudal society, appearing as a supplicant with hat in hand before the lords and kings of yesteryear, some elements of the Chinese bourgeoisie also learned to give voice to "official Marxism," singing the praises of communism and entering the party.

51) Certain pro-bourgeois forces, self-seekers and careerists viewed the now-ruling Communist Party as a vehicle for individual promotion. Not unlike the experience in the Soviet Union, also a country trying to use socialist methods to emerge from underdevelopment, pro-bourgeois elements infiltrated the Party. Their social and political weight influenced the views of long-standing communist leaders about the best path for China's development, which heightened their influence in society.

52) The Great Proletarian Cultural Revolution, initiated in 1966, was, in essence, an attempt by Mao and the left wing of the CPC to arrest the tendency of bourgeois and pro-bourgeois forces to gain control of the Communist Party of China. Their ascendancy in the party became evident in 1959 and 1960 following the failure of the Great Leap Forward, an effort to industrialize and emerge from underdevelopment by relying on the mobilization of the masses rather than resorting to capitalist methods.

In large part, this unconventional effort to create "backyard steel furnaces" throughout China was a radical response to the loss of Soviet economic aid and the precipitous and unprincipled removal of Soviet economic advisors in 1960 as retaliation for China's political opposition to the U.S.-Soviet accommodation. The Great Leap Forward led to severe dislocations and distortions and, ultimately, economic contraction. It also led to the removal of Mao from key posts and the ascension of those who were later labeled "capitalist roaders" during the Cultural Revolution.

The accusation that certain party leaders were "capitalist roaders" may have seemed to many as one more rhetorical flourish or excess of the Cultural Revolution. But the accusation, as it turned out, was not overheated rhetoric at all. It was a precise and accurate description of Mao's political opponents inside the leadership of the Communist Party. Following Mao's death in 1976, the left wing of the party was routed and its leaders were arrested. By 1978, the "capitalist roaders," galvanized under the leadership of Deng Xiaoping, introduced sweeping economic reforms under the newly concocted and theoretically unfounded label "market socialism."

53) The ascension of the right wing of the party did not signify a change in the class character of China. Self-described "Maoists" outside China immediately characterized China as a capitalist country. This characterization was as false as Mao's unscientific characterization in 1967 and 1968 of the Soviet Union as "capitalist" or "fascist" or "social-imperialist."

54) Saying that China is a fully capitalist country is politically disarming. It justifies standing on the sidelines or supporting imperialism in the inevitable confrontation between imperialism and the "socialist states"—a confrontation that is an organic and inescapable feature of the modern global class struggle. The confrontation rears its head regardless of the "sell out" or accomodationist orientation of the leaders.

In the international struggle, because of conflicting social and class interests, the interests of socialism, the working class and the states that emerged from socialist revolutions may be, and are, distorted and even mutilated by the orientation of leadership.

But these interests are not entirely extinguished. The proclamations of some on the "left" that this is not the case does not actually impact the imperialists' orientation and commitment toward counterrevolution, intervention and aggression aimed at the re-enslavement of peoples.

THE IMPORTANCE OF THE POLITICAL
CHARACTERIZATION: YUGOSLAVIA

55) The example of Yugoslavia is the most compelling evidence of this retrograde tendency on the left. It is also living proof of what is at stake. During the last four decades of the existence of the Soviet Union, U.S. imperialism acted in a more or less friendly way toward Yugoslavia. Although it was led by a Communist Party, Yugoslavia maintained "neutrality" in the U.S.-Soviet conflict. Yugoslavia's leadership introduced market reforms, largely abandoned the monopoly of foreign trade, integrated the country into the world capitalist economy, became heavily indebted to western banks, allowed large-scale unemployment to develop in accordance with the principle of the "market" and its need for a flexible labor pool, and began following the dictates of the International Monetary Fund. By the late 1980s, Yugoslavia was characterized by most of the left as a "capitalist country" with the clear implication that there was nothing remaining for the left to defend.

56) But because the League of Communists continued to hold onto power in Yugoslavia, it emerged as a force of resistance when German imperialism initiated a full-scale effort to dismember the country in 1990 and 1991. The overthrow of the East German socialist government in 1989 and its reincorporation into West Germany triggered an intense drive by German imperialism to enlarge its sphere of influence. It financed and secretly organized the secession of Slovenia and Croatia, the westernmost republics within multinational Yugoslavia. This in turn set off a predictable and classic imperialist scramble between Germany, France, England and finally the United States to carve up Yugoslavia into spheres of influence for neo-colonial penetration.

57) In the face of this imperialist-inspired counterrevolutionary campaign, the League of Communists, led by Slobodan Milosevic, abruptly changed course. Privatization of industry was slowed and in some cases reversed. Cooperation with the IMF was slowed or halted. Imperialism demonized the Yugoslav leadership, imposed economic sanctions and set on a course of regime change. Yugoslavia fought back against the forces of disintegration. It had to rely more on its working-class base. This would have been an impossible turn by a

fully capitalist regime, a regime that did not have its roots in social revolution and socialized property.

58) The only way for imperialism to succeed in Yugoslavia was to wage an all-out bombing war. From March 24 to June 4, 1999, NATO's collective imperialist air force dropped 23,000 bombs and missiles on Serbia until the Yugoslav government decided to let Kosovo go into the arms of the imperialists. Without pause, imperialist pressure intensified after the conclusion of the 1999 war to carry out the final counterrevolutionary ouster of the Yugoslav government and its replacement by a servile, proxy force.

59) Having long abandoned a political defense of Yugoslavia on the basis that there was nothing remaining, in the social and economic sense, from the initial Yugoslav revolution, big sections of the international left remained on the sidelines in 1999 watching the carnage. Others actually supported NATO's war or gave support to some variant form of imperialist-sponsored dismemberment, mouthing vulgarized proclamations about "self-determination" for Kosovo. Real self-determination, under those circumstances, meant only one thing: militantly defending the Yugoslav government as it resisted the imperialist aggression and the counterrevolution.

THE ORGANIC CONNECTION BETWEEN
IMPERIALISM AND COUNTERREVOLUTION

60) The Yugoslav example proves that there is an organic connection between imperialism and counterrevolution in all the societies with governments created by a socialist overturn.

61) Despite the emergence of conservative and non-revolutionary leaderships in the socialist-oriented governments, there has never been a long-term, stable partnership between any of these regimes and imperialism or any single imperialist government.

62) The very existence of a communist party as a ruling party—which is based on the interests of the working class—means that the relationship with imperialism is inherently unstable. The reason for the instability is that the mere hold on power by the communist parties constitutes an obstacle to the full and complete takeover and neo-colonial re-enslavement of the country by imperialism.

63) In its systematic and inherent quest for super profits, imperialism is driven towards counterrevolution with the principal objective

of overthrowing the political rule of the communist party. The thrust toward counterrevolution is in the very nature of the beast.

64) While Yugoslavia is one example of this counterrevolutionary phenomenon, one can look at recent Chinese history to observe a nearly identical process, most notably the events leading to the suppression of the Tiananmen Square counterrevolutionary movement in 1989. It was the leadership of the Communist Party of China, and in particular the leadership of Deng Xiaoping, who took steps to suppress a mass movement that occupied Tiananmen Square for seven weeks in 1989, the same year that most of the socialist bloc governments in Eastern Europe were overthrown.

THE TWOFOLD CHARACTER OF U.S. IMPERIALISM'S ATTITUDE TOWARD DENG XIAOPING AND THE 'CAPITALIST ROADERS'

65) Deng Xiaoping's government of "capitalist roaders" was cheered by the U.S. ruling class along with all the imperialist governments for opening up China to foreign investment starting in 1978. They all championed Deng and his grouping for introducing "market socialism." They all supported Deng for his discounting of Mao and the destruction of the Mao faction, as well as for the repudiation of the Cultural Revolution.

This process of "reform" led to the creation of a bourgeoisie, whose growing influence inside and outside the Communist Party sparked the Tiananmen Square movement, the success of which would have led to the dislodging of the Communist Party from power. So when the Deng Xiaoping-led government suppressed this movement, it became the subject of fierce attack by every imperialist country without exception. While the struggle was coming to a head in late May and in the first days of June 1989, every imperialist government, every one of their intelligence agencies and all of their international media outlets, without exception, coordinated support for the "student" resistance in Beijing, the capital and the seat of power of the government of the People's Republic China.

66) By comparison, it is impossible to find a single progressive student uprising anywhere in the capitalist world that gets even the faintest praise from even a small part of the imperialist establishment and the big business media, much less fully mobilized and

coordinated support from the major capitalist governments. Protests by privileged university students against Venezuelan president Hugo Chávez in Venezuela are cheered as the "voice of the people" because the imperialist media corporations understand the class orientation of these student protests—just as they did in China in 1989.

UNDER WHAT CIRCUMSTANCES DO WE POLITICALLY DEFEND THE CHINESE GOVERNMENT?: A BRIEF REVIEW OF THE REVOLUTIONARY APPROACH TOWARD THE SOVIET UNION

67) During the Soviet Union's years of existence, it was absolutely correct and imperative to militantly defend the Soviet social system in its confrontation with imperialist aggression and from the forces of internal bourgeois counterrevolution. This defense was just as earnest and militant whether one agreed or differed with the political positions of the Communist Party of the Soviet Union. In the case of the Soviet Union, we recognize that the workers' state had serious and innumerable flaws. We opposed, and still oppose, idealistic or uncritical support that pretends the Soviet Union was what its leaders said it was. That kind of idealistic and uncritical support for the Soviet leadership was a terrible flaw of the Communist Party USA and other Soviet-oriented parties. Every twist and turn made by the Soviet leadership, in both domestic and foreign policy, was unquestionably promoted by the CPUSA as a correct decision politically, which always corresponded exactly, the story went, to the needs of the Soviet Union and the international working-class movement.

68) In the case of the Maoist followers of the Communist Party of China, the same method of uncritical acceptance and support for the Chinese leadership was the rule. In both instances, this kind of idealistic defense made the ideological camp followers of both the Soviet and Chinese parties extremely vulnerable. The sudden turns and shifts of the Soviet and Chinese parties seemed utterly contradictory to positions and policies that the parties had been invoking as the "correct" position just before these same positions were abandoned. All in all, this method was politically disarming and led to many losses inside the movement. Idealism, suffering moral setbacks when it comes into contact with reality, turns into its very opposite—

cynicism. Cynicism is anathema to revolutionary vision, devouring the revolutionary energy of many earnest and honest activists.

69) Critical support for a flawed workers' state was first developed in relation to the Soviet Union. In the course of that analysis, an established criterion for evaluating the class character of the social relations was developed. Since support was being offered unstintingly to the social system, to the workers' state as a new social formation, rather than to the positions and policies of the leadership, it is useful to examine that criterion as we articulate our stance toward China today.

Is it the same criterion, or are there additional factors to take into account? All analogies are by their nature inexact. No two things are really the same. All generalized experience, which we would place under the broad category called "theory," is based on what has come before. It would not have been possible to adopt a method, an orientation or a theory about the formation of a bureaucratically flawed workers' state until the real-life formation of the Soviet Union and the problems it faced. Marxism is not a philosophy in the sense of adopting a closed world view about how things should be or will be. It uses the scientific method, investigating reality and deriving truth from facts. Theory is a guide, not a closed system. It is not a dogma that attempts to explain all social phenomena in a supra-historical way. We have to use this method when analyzing China as it is.

WHAT IS A WORKERS' STATE?

70) There were four basic features of the Soviet Union that constituted the foundation for the Soviet workers' state, which despite its bureaucratic flaws and deformities distinguished it as a viable and superior social system in comparison to the capitalist system that preceded it in Russia.

First, the state and government were created following the smashing of the old state power of the bourgeoisie by a revolution of the workers and peasants. Second, there was public ownership of the means of production. Third, there was centralized economic planning rather than the commodity market as the engine driving economic production. This might be summarized as production to meet needs rather than derive private profit. Fourth, the government administered a monopoly of foreign trade.

71) During most of its 74 years, the Soviet Union maintained these key features and they shaped the economic system following the 1917 workers' and peasants' revolution. It is what distinguished the Soviet system from the capitalist mode of production. It was not a fully developed socialist system. On the contrary, it could be argued that the Soviet Union never evolved past the very first stage of socialist "social relations." There was inequality and many hangovers of underdevelopment. Economic and social underdevelopment was the most striking feature of Russia and the other Soviet Republics during the early period of the Soviet Union.

72) But the Soviet Union was clearly functioning according to an economic mechanism that was far different from the capitalist market and production based on private profit. Using these preliminary socialist economic methods, the Soviet Union developed into the second-largest economy in the world. It eliminated unemployment. This system had no need for an industrial reserve army of the unemployed because production was no longer based on squeezing surplus value out of the working class. The paramount requirement to satisfy the profit needs of the capitalist and investor class was gone because the capitalists were deposed as a ruling class.

73) Using this non-capitalist mode of production, the Soviet Union did not just grow into a major world power. Soviet workers and peasants achieved unheard of social and economic rights and benefits. These rights were legal rights, rights the state defended rather than defending the right of capital to exploit labor. For the first time in history, the so-called "rule of law" was applied to the needs of the oppressed class for employment, housing, health care, education, child care, recreation and relaxation.

THE 'LOGIC' OF THE CAPITALIST MARKET

74) Until the start of the "economic reforms" in 1978, the Chinese economy was functioning more or less in accordance with the four principal and distinctive non-capitalist mechanisms that were foundational to the Soviet economy, including public ownership of the factories, banking and transport and collectivized farming in the countryside.

The pro-capitalist economic reforms have continued since 1978 in successive stages. These different stages sometimes accelerated in the direction of all-out restoration of unfettered capitalist relations, while at other times slowing this trend. In general, however, there can be no dispute of the fact that the Chinese economy is today being increasingly driven by the "logic" of the capitalist market, including the global capitalist market.

This increasing integration is partly by design and partly because the capitalist market has its own "logic." Each economic reform contains within itself its own contradictions for China. Those who seek to manage the market are also managed by the market and by the underlying fact that in a market-driven economy, capital is king. Capital flows to where profit can be maximized in a system based on ruthless competition. A "flexible labor pool," as the capitalists put it so blandly, requires workers who can be fired and hired when needed—as the "market" demands. Maximizing profit means removing government, labor and environmental rights and restrictions that obstruct unfettered investment and profit taking. If China wants to succeed in the global capitalist market, it must play by the rules of economic globalization, or capital will flow to other countries.

75) During the last 29 years, China has incrementally reorganized its economy. Public ownership still exists in large parts of the industrial sector, in what are called state-owned enterprises, but there is at this moment an increasing tilt toward privatization. The meaning of the statistics on the real level of public ownership is not easily discernible from a distance. Property forms can be called private when they are still actually state run in the public sector and vice versa. But what is not in dispute is that the trend is toward more and more privatization of publicly owned enterprises and banks. The monopoly of foreign trade has been gradually reduced and there are an untold number of direct economic links between Chinese enterprises and transnational imperialist corporations. The state is still a major force in managing resource allocation and granting or preventing access to the Chinese market, but its formal state-based decision process must also be largely driven by the "logic" of economic globalization and the needs of foreign investment capital. And this "logic," regardless of whether it is dictating the decisions of planners in the state-owned enterprises or in the private sectors, is antithetical to the interests of the working class. The market and the need to prove profitability lead to layoffs, the diminution of benefits, etc.

CHINA'S BARGAINING CHIP

76) The Communist Party of China is operating according to the assumption that this is the only—or at least the fastest—method to acquire the technology that is critical to China's long-term rise from underdevelopment to becoming a medium-developed country by the middle of the 20th century. This is their goal. The underlying calculation of the Deng Xiaoping wing of the "capitalist roader" faction of the party is that if the Communist Party of China can retain its hold on supreme political power it can manage the capital investment rather than having the country plunged into neo-colonial or semi-colonial slavery. The basis for this assessment is that while China is weak in comparison to the imperialist states and the transnational mega-corporations and banks, it has something to strengthen its hand in negotiating the terms of capital investment and foreign direct investment. That something is the sheer size of the Chinese market, and most of all the potential Chinese market, and the sheer size of the potential Chinese industrial labor pool employable at low wages that can be hired by transnationals for the production of export goods sold on the world market. The Chinese domestic market could easily dwarf all of Europe within just a few decades, and this is a card that can be played in negotiating the terms of technology transfer, types of investment and forms of partnership.

77) The Communist Party of China's thinking is that the "prize" of access to China's market and its vast low-wage labor pool are sufficient to give the government bargaining power so that foreign direct investment is also harnessed to benefit China's development plans and to improve the standard of living of sizeable sectors of the population by gaining greater access to technology and consumer goods. This is not only premised on the liquidation of the monopoly of foreign trade, public ownership and directed, centralized economic planning, it is also based on the elimination of the codified rights of the working class and peasantry, rights that made China one of the most egalitarian societies between 1952 and 1978.

MYTHS ABOUT CHINA'S ROLE IN THE WORLD ECONOMY

78) As we examine the issue of the social and class character of China today, as we attempt to put its pro-capitalist economic reforms into a larger perspective, it is important to have a true sense of China's role in the world economy. The reports in the mass media

have painted a false picture. China has certainly increased its role in the global economy, but it is entirely misleading to characterize China as the new economic superpower.

79) China has a population of 1.3 billion people—that is, 1 billion more people than the United States—but its economy is one-seventh the size of the U.S. economy and one-third the size of the Japanese economy.[11] In per capita income, "China remains a low income country, ranked roughly 100th in the world."[12] In 1978, China accounted for less than 1 percent of the world economy, while today it accounts for 4 percent.[13]

80) The constant commentary that "everything is made in China" these days is designed to give the impression that China generates—and possesses—a huge section of the world's wealth derived from industrial production. This too is wrong.

81) Figures are routinely cited showing that the bilateral trade deficit between the United States and China is growing wildly. But the data on bilateral trade is misleading. Transnational corporations own most of the products that have the "Made in China" label, and many of them are U.S.-based corporations. These products are often designed elsewhere. Their components are produced elsewhere and then shipped to China for the final stage of assembly. Then they are "exported" from China back to the United States, Japan and Europe. Since they leave China last, these internationally produced commodities have a "Made in China" tag. But China doesn't get the profits, since the exported products belong to the transnational imperialist corporations. China frequently does not receive significant technology transfer either with the exception of the "assembly" factory.

82) Under these arrangements, China derives revenue from the wages paid to factory workers who might otherwise be unemployed or living in traditional poverty as peasants. "The biggest beneficiary of this is the United States. A Barbie doll costs $20 but China only gets 35 cents of that," said Dong Tao, a Hong Kong-based economist.[14] Sixty percent of China's exports are actually controlled by foreign companies, according to Chinese customs data.[15]

THE STRIPPING OF ECONOMIC AND SOCIAL RIGHTS

83) While workers in the state sector of the economy have extensive social security protections, the rights of workers in the expanding private sector are far less generous. Unemployed workers

from the non-state sector do not have secure access to housing and health care. The decision to de-emphasize the rural economy has forced millions of Chinese peasants to leave the countryside for the urban centers. This insecure and migrant labor pool has been the basis for the vast pool of low-wage workers that foreign investors are trying to exploit. Thousands of assembly factories established by the transnational corporations have employed millions of these migrant laborers for about 75 cents an hour.[16]

84) China's economic development strategy based on the "opening up" of the country has stimulated the growth of an internal bourgeoisie and middle class. It has provided more disposable income for a large number of urbanized factory workers. But an untold number of Chinese workers and peasants have been cast into an existence that is fraught with the insecurity reminiscent of the European proletariat at an earlier stage of the industrial revolution between 100 and 150 years ago.

85) The "opening up" of China has benefited U.S. and foreign corporations greatly. This new and expanding capital market has given a huge boost to the short-term stability of global capitalism—a boost that may quickly turn into its opposite, given the logic of the capitalist economic cycle. But China's leaders believe that this path over the long term is the fastest way to modernize the productive forces and allow China to overcome its status as an underdeveloped country. The massive factory build up has in fact led to an accelerated creation of cities and a new urban existence for tens of millions of former rural dwellers throughout China. The leadership believes that over time the Chinese people will accrue the technical skills and the technology base to "catch up" with the advanced capitalist countries.

COMPARING CHINA AND THE SOVIET UNION

86) China, since the 1978 reforms, has embarked on a development path distinct from the Soviet economic model. While the state is still under the leadership of the Communist Party of China, as the Communist Party of the Soviet Union led the Soviet state, the Soviet model up until its collapse in 1991 was based on the dominance of public ownership, centralized planning and the monopoly of foreign trade.

87) The sociological definition of the Soviet state as a workers' state, albeit one with major deformations and flaws, was based

on this objective criterion. Does this definition apply to the People's Republic of China?

THE CHINESE STATE HAS ASSUMED MANY OF THE TASKS OF A BOURGEOIS STATE

88) Both China and the former Soviet Union consisted of states and governments that were birthed by a workers and peasants revolution, with a proletarian (communist) party at the helm. Both used a similar economic model with the perspective of building socialism and not capitalism over the long term. Socialism was the perspective.

89) Since the economic reforms of 1978, China has incrementally and radically shifted its economic model away from socialist methods in order to integrate its national economy into the world capitalist economy.

90) These reforms have given rise to a new bourgeoisie inside China. The state, led by the Communist Party of China, has functioned as the protector of this bourgeoisie both in its relations with the Chinese working class and in its relations with the imperialist bourgeoisie.

91) To the extent that the Chinese state has promoted and enforced the rights, the interests and the needs of the Chinese bourgeoisie and the transnational corporations functioning within China, the state assumes the tasks of a bourgeois state. Since it is a state that originated from a working-class revolution and enjoyed an immense base of support from within the working class and peasantry, the Chinese state has only been able incrementally and over a time frame of several decades to diminish its historic obligations and defense of its original social base.

92) The Chinese state, including the Communist Party of China, has essential elements of what is known as Bonapartism, meaning the ruling party has to a degree straddled the class divide and has a foot in the camps of the bourgeoisie and the working class. The actual living experience of China in its evolution since 1949 is without precedent. Its differences with the Soviet Union's evolution require us to acknowledge that it is not an exactly analogous social formation at this point.

93) The destruction and incremental dissolution of public ownership, centralized planning and the monopoly of foreign trade

constitutes a historic setback for the Chinese working class. Its rights and interests have either been stripped or seriously eroded while the rights of capital, including foreign capital, have been elevated.

94) The advancement of the Chinese bourgeoisie has been at the expense of the political and social primacy of the working class. To the extent that a larger section of the Chinese population, including the working class, has additional access to goods, it comes as a form of personal or individual acquisition and cannot mask the fact that the status of the working class as a class has been seriously downgraded in terms of its social rights and political weight within the state and party.

95) Of course, capitalist social relations in China are progressive in relation to feudal or semi-feudal relations. But they are retrogressive in comparison to the relations achieved by the proletariat and peasantry in the first decades following the victory of the revolution.

96) The label of "market socialism" obscures what is taking place in China. This purported hybrid between two social systems is a theoretical fiction—really a theoretical caricature of Marxism. Socialism is the next stage of human society after capitalism. The wealth of society created under the capitalist system is made public and the forces of production are set into motion to meet human needs. The market belongs to the era of commodity exchange, to the production and distribution of social wealth according to class privilege and class interests. The capitalist market, based on making profit, and socialist production, based on satisfying need, are mutually antagonistic methods for the organization of production. Beneath the surface, this antagonism between two contradictory methods of production and distribution are the irreconcilable contradictions between the working class and the bourgeoisie.

THE BOURGEOIS AND PROLETARIAN REVOLUTIONS

97) The socialist revolutions in Russia in 1917 and later in Korea, China, Vietnam, Cuba and elsewhere catapulted the working class to the position of the ruling class. In all of these countries, however, the revolution by necessity was forced to complete the fundamental tasks of both the bourgeois democratic and the socialist proletarian revolutions. Because the seizure of power did not take place in the advanced capitalist countries that had for the most part enjoyed a prolonged stage of post-feudal bourgeois social and economic development, the

new revolutionary governments were confronted with the delayed, unfinished and sometimes unstarted tasks that the bourgeoisie had already accomplished in Western Europe.

98) The break-up of semi-feudal and feudal relations in the countryside, the introduction of mechanized agriculture, the urbanization of the population, the introduction of large-scale manufacture, mass literacy and the introduction of bourgeois culture in contrast to the rustic rural-based patriarchy—these were revolutionary tasks that the bourgeoisie carried out in Western Europe, first inside the confines of the old feudal order where the bourgeoisie functioned as an oppressed class, and later as it mounted a struggle for political power and became a ruling class throughout Europe. In England and France the bourgeois revolution against the old feudal order was carried out in the 1600s and 1700s, respectively.

99) The triumph of Western European, U.S. and Japanese colonialist and imperialist domination had the effect of retarding the ability of the bourgeoisie, as a class, in the colonized, semi-feudal and feudal world from carrying out the same historic mission and tasks. Thus, the socialist revolution in the underdeveloped countries had to carry out both the tasks associated with the bourgeois democratic revolution and the socialist reorganization of society.

100) Because of this underdevelopment enforced by imperialism, the advanced productive forces that Marx considered to be a prerequisite for the socialist stage of society were missing in the oppressed world. The working-class revolutions, as they began on the road toward socialist collectivization, were faced with the even more primary challenge of how to build up the productive forces just to feed hungry people; to provide housing, rudimentary elementary and secondary education, and electrification to the entire country; to build basic roads and other core infrastructure; and so forth. These are the social tasks that historically belong to the era of the bourgeois revolution. Moreover, in this tortured social environment, the new revolutionary governments in underdeveloped countries not only had to confront the forces of domestic counterrevolution, but the combined force of world imperialism. The imperialists employed and continue to employ almost limitless resources to threaten, subvert, sanction, invade and overthrow these new revolutionary governments.

101) The Chinese government and the Communist Party of China have turned increasingly toward reliance on bourgeois and

capitalist methods—rather than on the socialist methods of the Mao era—to pursue the completion of the tasks of China's bourgeois democratic revolution. This struggle to overcome underdevelopment and see China rise as a modern economic power on the world stage is part and parcel of the bourgeois democratic revolution.

102) It is a historical irony that China's socialist revolution was the essential guarantor for the qualitative advance of the bourgeois democratic revolution, and for the growth of a non-comprador bourgeois class in China. All the governments that came before 1949 left China to be ravaged by colonialism and imperialism working with and through Chinese comprador proxies.

WHERE WE STAND:
DEFEND CHINA AGAINST COUNTERREVOLUTION, IMPERIALIST INTERVENTION AND DISMEMBERMENT

103) To the extent that the policies of the Chinese state have undermined the socialist aspirations of the working class in favor of the rights and interests of the Chinese non-comprador bourgeoisie, they must be viewed as a regressive step. As communists, we oppose those policies and look toward those Chinese communists who are trying to reverse them. However, to the extent that this same Chinese state functions as a nationally unifying force defending China's forward march in completing the tasks of the bourgeois democratic revolution, staving off the marauding reflexes and designs of world imperialism and the transnational corporations, we also recognize that the overthrow of the Chinese government and the political rule of the Communist Party by any force other than a vanguard communist party will inevitably result in a tragic defeat and setback for the Chinese working class and for the nation and people as a whole.

104) The dialectical reality of the intertangling of the socialist revolution and the bourgeois democratic revolution has been the source of great confusion in the left, including among some of China's historic supporters.

105) On one side, the policies of the Communist Party of China are embraced by some on the left worldwide, including inside of North Korea, Vietnam and to some extent inside of Cuba as well. These forces consider "market socialism" to have been a creative and necessary innovation. After all, they say, the Communist Party of the

Soviet Union, with its "rigid" economic centralism, has been over-thrown, while the Chinese party continues in power and is managing an impressive economic rise from the margins of the world economy to its center. While acknowledging the growing class polarization in China, these advocates of "market socialism" argue that this is the price of economic integration and greater access to modern technology at the very moment that there is a global "high tech" revolution. According to these socialists, it is either integrate or fall behind.

106) On the other side are those in the left who have come to the position that the restoration of capitalism in China is complete, that there is nothing remaining to defend, that the Chinese government and the Communist Party are capitalist oppressors, and that all resistance to the regime is valid. Some organizations, like the International Socialist Organization, had this position even when China was relying on socialist methods. But there are also a large number of Maoists and former Maoists, people who earnestly defended China, who have now concluded that China is not fundamentally different from any other capitalist country. They offer no political support for China, almost regardless of circumstances.

107) For our part, we consider the words "market" and "socialism" to be contradictory. All the socialist countries have resorted to a limited use of the capitalist market at times, including the Soviet Union, which employed these measures during the New Economic Policy launched in 1921 while Lenin was still giving direction to the party. But these measures were considered an economic retreat to overcome famine and poverty so stark that it actually disbursed the urban proletariat back to the countryside in order to acquire food. Socialist relations did not exist, nor could they have in the economic chaos following World War I, the imperialist intervention and civil war. What is happening in China is fundamentally different. This is not a temporary retreat but a long-term policy of de-socialization of already nationalized and collectivized property. It is turning this property over to a class of capitalists. Under the label of "market socialism," it is the restoration of capitalist social relations.

The restoration of capitalist economic relations has been incremental and so far incomplete. It has not come about as the result of a counterrevolutionary overturn of the government. It is a process rather than an event. Although it is impossible to say with 100 percent certainty where in this process China is, it is indisputable that its basic trend has only deepened since 1978. This process is, however, unfinished. As long as the Communist Party of China retains its hold on political power, there is the possibility, however great or small, that this trend can be reversed. It could also be slowed or stalled in the face of unanticipated developments, such as a global capitalist economic crisis that would likely shake China's export-driven economy to its core, an internal class or intra-class confrontation, or even a large-scale confrontation with U.S. or Japanese imperialism. Again, it is imperative to keep in mind the example of what happened in Yugoslavia between 1989 and 1999, when the Yugoslav communists changed course in the face of imperialist intervention, dismemberment and internal civil war.

108) To the extent that workers and peasants in China rebel or resist capitalist encroachments and abuses, we should show solidarity with their struggle—especially to the extent that these protests lead toward reversing the gains of capital. The rightful place of the Communist Party of China is to stand with these workers and peasants in their confrontation with the Chinese government and with the domestic and foreign capitalists. If the communists stand aside, they will lose all credibility with their historic social base.

109) To the extent that these struggles, absent the leadership and support from the Communist Party, change from spontaneous battles for economic and social justice to movements that have been taken over politically by a leadership that seeks to overthrow the political rule of the Communist Party, these struggles will inevitably, under the current political circumstances, move into the camp of reactionary counterrevolution and will be organically connected to and nourished by the forces of world imperialism.

The overthrow of the Communist Party will lead not only to the absolute destruction of what is remaining of the old socialist revolution, but to the suspension of China's bourgeois democratic revolution—unless that overthrow is led by a national force committed to the interests of the working class against capitalism and imperialism. There is no indication that such a force exists today in China, although there certainly must be elements among the 73 million members of the Communist Party of China that support the revolutionary road of Mao Zedong and the Chinese socialist revolution.

The overthrow of the Communist Party of China by non-revolutionary forces would hurl China backward in its epoch-making struggle to emerge from underdevelopment. The overthrow of the Communist Party under those circumstances would return China to the semi-slavery of comprador neo-colonial rule. China would then also face the possibility of splintering, as happened in Yugoslavia and as may happen in Iraq under the impact of foreign occupation.

In the face of this threat, our Party would offer militant political defense of the Chinese government in spite of our profound differences with so-called "market socialism." □

Endnotes

1. Maurice Meisner, *The Deng Xiaoping Era: An Inquiry into the Fate of Chinese Socialism, 1978-1994* (Hill and Wang, 1996), 189; Mobo C.F. Gao, "Debating the Cultural Revolution—Do We Only Know What We Believe," *Critical Asian Studies,* vol. 34 no.3 (2002), 424-5.

2. Martin Hart-Landsberg and Paul Burkett, *China and Socialism: Market Reforms and Class Struggle,* (Monthly Review Press, 2005.)

3. Meisner, *The Deng Xiaoping Era,* 192.

4. Ibid., 193

5. Zheng Bijian, *Ten Views on China's Development Road of Peaceful Rise and Sino European Relations,* December 15, 2005.

6. Ibid.

7. Ibid.

8. Wang Jisi, "China's Search for Stability With America," *Foreign Affairs,* September/October 2005.

9. Ibid.

10. Ibid.

11. Zheng Bijian, "China's Peaceful Rise," *Foreign Affairs,* September/October 2005.

12. Ibid.

13. Ibid.

14. David Barboza, "Some Assembly Needed: China as Asia Factory," *New York Times,* February 9, 2006.

15. Ibid.

16. Ibid.

What is the Party for Socialism and Liberation?

The Party for Socialism and Liberation is a working-class party of leaders and activists from many different struggles, founded to promote the movement for revolutionary change.

There is only one solution to the crisis posed by state monopoly capitalism: socialism. To secure lasting peace and justice requires abolishing the dictatorship of the super-rich and their warfare state.

We stand for the socialist reorganization of society. There is no "third way." Illusions about a "kinder, gentler" capitalism are just that—illusions. The idea that the bosses and the capitalist state's grip on society can be abolished through any means other than a revolutionary overturn is utopian fantasy.

Revolutionary Marxism requires a revolutionary party to flourish and develop. Marxism is not an abstract doctrine but rather a guide to action. It must be constantly tested by action and in debate.

The PSL seeks to bring together leaders and organizers from the many struggles taking place across the country. The most crucial requirement for membership is the dedication to undertake this most important and most necessary of all tasks—building a new revolutionary workers party in the heart of world imperialism.

**To join the Party for Socialism and Liberation,
see the contacts page or visit www.PSLweb.org**

CONTACT THE PARTY FOR SOCIALISM AND LIBERATION

NATIONAL OFFICES

San Francisco, CA
sf@pslweb.org
2969 Mission St., Suite 200
San Francisco, CA 94110
415-821-6171

Washington, DC
dc@pslweb.org
PO Box 26451
Washington, DC 20001
202-234-2828

BRANCHES

Albuquerque, NM
abq@pslweb.org
505-503-3067

Austin, TX
austin@pslweb.org
512-577-4749

Baltimore MD
baltimore@pslweb.org
443-378-925

Boston, MA
boston@pslweb.org

Chicago, IL
chicago@pslweb.org
773-920-7590

Long Beach, CA
lb@pslweb.org

Los Angeles, CA
la@pslweb.org
323-810-3380

Miami, FL
miami@pslweb.org
305-710-3189

New Haven, CT
ct@pslweb.org
203-416-8365

New Paltz, NY
np@pslweb.org

New York City, NY
nyc@pslweb.org
212-694-8762

Philadelphia, PA
philly@pslweb.org

San Diego CA
sandiego@pslweb.org

San Jose, CA
sanjose@pslweb.org
408-829-9507

Seattle, WA
seattle@pslweb.org
206-367-3820

Syracuse, NY
syracuse@pslweb.org

for a complete listing visit PSLweb.org

Program of the
Party for Socialism and Liberation

Socialism and Liberation in the United States
outlines the basic political and
ideological positions of the Party
for Socialism and Liberation, a
revolutionary Marxist party in the
United States. The book describes
the basis for a united, working-
class struggle against imperialism,
a system that imperils the lives
and livelihoods of the majority of
people in the United States and
across the globe. *Socialism and
Liberation in the United States*
envisions a socialist future based
upon principles of workers'
democracy, cooperation, equality,
solidarity and sustainability. It
argues that the workers who
produce all of society's wealth
should own and control it.

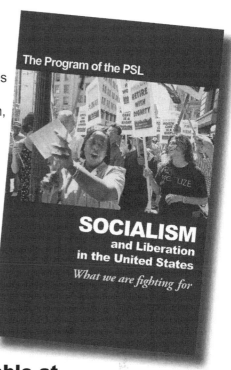

Available at
PSLprogram.org • PSLweb.org
and as e-books at
Amazon.com • BN.com

Paperback, 57 pages, $6.95.
November 2010
ISBN: 978-0-9841220-2-8
Library of Congress: 2010937412

PSL Publications
2969 Mission St. #200
San Francisco, CA 94110
books@PSLweb.org
(415) 821-6171

PALESTINE
Israel and
the U.S. Empire
by Richard Becker

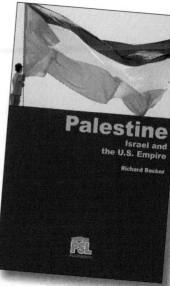

This book provides a sharp analysis of the
struggle for Palestine—from the division of
the Middle East by Western powers and the
Zionist settler movement, to the founding
of Israel and its role as a watchdog for
U.S. interests, to present-day conflicts and
the prospects for a just resolution. The
narrative is firmly rooted in the politics of
Palestinian liberation. Here is a necessary
contribution to the heroic efforts of the Palestinian people to
achieve justice in the face of seemingly insurmountable odds.

RICHARD BECKER is a writer and commentator on Middle East affairs.
He has visited the Middle East on numerous occasions, contributed to books
and videos on Iraq and Middle East affairs, and been a featured speaker
across the country and around the world.

*"Becker gives us the most focused and penetrating analysis we have of the
real dynamics in the continuing persecution of the Palestinian people."*
—**Ramsey Clark,** *former U.S. attorney general*

*"This book is a clarion call to end the last vestiges
of colonialism in the 21st century."*
—**Imam Mahdi Bray,** *executive director, Muslim American Society Freedom*

"A must-read for anyone seeking to understand the Palestinian cause."
—**Samera Sood,** *executive board,*
Palestinian American Women's Association

*"Becker foregrounds what others usually set aside: the integral role
of U.S. imperialism, with the Zionist State as an essential partner."*
—**Joel Kovel,** *author, "Overcoming Zionism"*

Paperback, 233 pages, illustrated, indexed. Price: $17.95
ISBN: 978-0-9841220-0-4, October 2009, PSL Publications

Available at PalestineBook.com and PSLweb.org
Also on Amazon

68277201R00120